Brief Spanish Reference Grammar

Brief Spanish Reference Grammar

Roman Colbert
SANTA MONICA COLLEGE

 D. Van Nostrand Company

New York Cincinnati Toronto London Melbourne

D. Van Nostrand Company Regional Offices:
New York   Cincinnati   Millbrae

D. Van Nostrand Company International Offices:
London   Toronto   Melbourne

Copyright © 1975 by Litton Educational Publishing, Inc.

Library of Congress Catalog Card Number: 74-10493

ISBN: 0-442-21616-5

Published by D. Van Nostrand Company
450 West 33rd Street, New York, N.Y. 10001

Published simultaneously in Canada by
Van Nostrand Reinhold Ltd.

10 9 8 7 6 5 4 3 2 1

Preface

Brief Spanish Reference Grammar has been designed to present the basic concepts of Spanish grammar in an easily accessible format. It is intended to serve as a convenient reference handbook and is therefore not exhaustive in treatment. The book is especially useful in courses emphasizing reading and/or conversation, where a full review grammar is not wanted.

In order to avoid the complexities inherent in detailed grammar manuals, the author has aimed to provide:

1. A tool for instructors to refer students easily to pertinent grammar problems.
2. A concise but thorough review and reference guide for students.
3. A practical format for quick and easy location of rules and examples.
4. Complete listing of verbs, including regular, irregular, reflexive, orthographical-changing, radical-changing, and those requiring prepositions.
5. Useful lists of cognates and deceptive cognates, idiomatic expressions, impersonal expressions, expressions of quantity, prepositions, conjunctions, and others.
6. A comprehensive index designed to facilitate reference and review.

This book contains no grammar exercises, drills, or translation passages. No attempt has been made to make it conform to the characteristic patterns of a standard review grammar. It is strictly a reference guide enabling the student to learn or review the basic Spanish grammar rules and to master their difficulties.

Contents

Brief Spanish Reference Grammar

1 Los artículos

1.1 El artículo indefinido **un, una, unos, unas** (Indefinite article)

Indefinite articles refer to objects or persons not specifically identified.

MASC.	**un** libro	*a book*	**unos** libros	*some books*
FEM.	**una** silla	*a chair*	**unas** sillas	*some chairs*

In Spanish, the indefinite article is generally not used:

A. Before an unmodified predicate noun (that is, after **ser**) denoting occupation, nationality, and religious or political affiliation.

Es americano.   **Son católicos.**   **Es comunista.**
Es médico.   **Es judía.**   **Eran republicanos.**

But:

Es **un** protestante ferviente.   Es **un** médico de fama mundial.

B. Before **otro** *another,* **cierto** *certain,* **medio** *half,* **cien** *a hundred,* **mil** *a thousand,* and after **tal** *such a* and **qué** *what a.* Note that the English equivalents include the article.

medio mundo   ¡Qué lástima!   hace **mil años**
Nunca se ha visto **tal cosa.**   ¿Tiene **otra pregunta** ?

But:

un ciento de   *a hundred of*   **un** millón de   *a million of*

C. After a negative.

No tengo papel.   *I haven't any paper.*
No hemos comprado casa todavía.   *We haven't bought a house yet.*

D. After the preposition **sin.**

Salió **sin dinero.**   una mujer **sin cabeza**

[1]

E.   **Un** is used before feminine singular nouns beginning with a stressed **a** or **ha**.

un alma   un hacha

1.2 El artículo definido **el, la, los, las** (Definite article)

MASC.	**el** libro	*the book*	**los** libros	*the books*
FEM.	**la** ventana	*the window*	**las** ventanas	*the windows*

The definite article indicates a definite thing or person.

el libro del profesor	*the professor's book*
la camisa de Juan	*John's shirt*
los estudiantes de la clase	*the students of the class*
las cartas de su madre	*his (her, your, their) mother's letters*

The definite article is used:

A.   To designate a general class, an entire category of persons, or a general concept. In these cases, the definite article is not normally used in English.

El dinero es necesario.	*Money is necessary.*
Los libros son útiles.	*Books are useful.*
Me gustan **los perros**.	*I like dogs.*

B.   Before names of languages, except when they follow **en, de,** or the verb **hablar.** After verbs such as **estudiar, aprender, escribir,** and **entender,** the definite article may be used or omitted.

El francés es difícil.
French is difficult.

Estudian **el francés** todos los días.
They study French every day.

Ella me dice **en inglés** que **habla español.**
She tells me in English that she (he) speaks Spanish.

Su profesor **de alemán** es antipático.
His (her, your, their) German professor is unpleasant.

After **traducir de** and **venir de,** the article is used.

El español **viene del latín.**
Spanish comes from Latin.

Este libro fue **traducido del inglés.**
This book was translated from English.

C. Before all titles, except in direct address.

La señora Álvarez   **el capitán Mendoza**
el presidente Kennedy   **el doctor Marañón**

But:

—Buenas tardes, **señor Valdés.**

D. To express dates.

el 16 de septiembre   **el 4 de julio**

E. With the day of the week to express recurrence of an action or state, or to refer to a particular day.

Voy a la iglesia **los domingos.**
I go to church on Sundays.

Este restaurante está cerrado **los lunes.**
This restaurant is closed on Mondays.

el sábado próximo
next Saturday

F. With the time of day.

Son **las tres** de la mañana.   *It is three o'clock in the morning.*
Es **la una y media.**   *It is one thirty.*

G. With parts of the body. Note that the possessive adjective is used in English.

Me duele **la cabeza.**   *My head hurts.*
Se lavaron **las manos.**   *They washed their hands.*

H. With articles of clothing when the possessor has been previously identified.

Me quité **el sombrero.**   *I took off my hat.*
Se puso **los zapatos.**   *He (she) put on his (her) shoes.*

I. The definite article is not used before **don, doña, San, Santo,** and **Santa.**

Don Juan   **Doña** Inés   **Santa** María   **San** Francisco

J.   The definite article is generally repeated before each noun.

      Tengo **el** libro, **el** papel y **el** lápiz.

K.   **El** is used before feminine singular nouns beginning with a stressed **a** or **ha**.

      el agua   el alma   el hambre

1.3 Las contracciones del artículo definido: **al, del** (Contractions with the definite article)

When the prepositions **de** or **a** precede the article **el**, they contract with it.

de + el = del   *of the, from the*
a   + el = al   *to the, at the*

el discurso **del** presidente
El sábado iremos **al** teatro.

1.4 El artículo neutro **lo** (Neuter article **lo**)

A.   The neuter article **lo** is used before adjectives and past participles to form nouns.

      Lo difícil es perseverar.   *The difficulty is to persevere.*
      Lo indicado es comer poco.   *The right thing to do is eat little.*

B.   The form **lo** + adverb + **que** is used to express the English *how* + adverb.

      ¿Ven **lo rápidamente que** aprenden?   *Do you see how fast they learn?*

2 La interrogación

2.1 Any statement may be converted into a question by placing the subject pronoun (if one is used) immediately after the verb. An inverted question mark is placed immediately before the question.

¿Fueron ustedes con él?   **¿Se mudó ella** de casa?

If the subject is a noun which is as long as, or longer than, the object, it is placed at the end of the question.

¿Habla **español el amigo de tu padre?**
Does your father's friend speak Spanish?

An adverb such as **mucho** or **bien** is placed before the subject.

¿Trabajan **mucho** los estudiantes?
Do the students work a lot?

2.2 If additional information is sought, the following interrogative words can start the sentence.

     A.   Adjectives (See also *Los adjetivos interrogativos 4.3.*)

         ¿qué?   **¿Qué hora es?**
         ¿cuánto (-a, -os, -as)?   **¿Cuántos libros tiene usted?**

     B.   Pronouns (See also *Los pronombres interrogativos 18.6.*)

         ¿qué?   **¿cuánto (-a, -os, -as)?**   **¿quién (-es)?**   **¿cuál (-es)?**
         ¿Qué hay en la caja?   **¿Quién** es usted?   **¿De quién** hablas?

     C.   Adverbs (See also *La formación de los adverbios 6.1H.*)

         ¿dónde?   **¿cómo?**   **¿adónde?**   **¿por qué?**   **¿cuándo?**
         ¿De dónde es usted?   **¿Cómo** se llama usted?   **¿Cuándo** vamos al cine?

2.3 The interrogative word always has a written accent. In indirect discourse, the interrogative word retains the written accent.

Alicia me preguntó **adónde** y con **quién** íbamos.
Alice asked me where and with whom we were going.

3 La negación

3.1 El uso de **no** (Use of **no**)

A. Sentences are made negative by placing **no** before the entire verb form.

No hablo con ella.	*I don't speak to her.*
No hemos ido.	*We didn't go.*
No estaban estudiando.	*They were not studying.*

B. Only object pronouns may be placed between **no** and the verb form. (See also *Los pronombres 18.1G.*)

No **se lo** diré.	*I will not tell it to him (her, you, them).*
No **la** hemos visto.	*We have not seen her (or it).*
No **me** hagas caso.	*Don't pay attention to me.*

C. **No** is placed at the end of a sentence without a verb.

¿Viene con nosotros?	Ella sí, él **no.**
Is he (she) coming with us?	*She is, he isn't.*
¿Te gusta el pescado?	A mí **no.** Hoy **no.**
Do you like the fish?	*I don't.* *Today I don't.*

3.2 Las palabras negativas y afirmativas (Negative and affirmative words)

nunca, jamás	*never, not ever*	**siempre**	*always*
		a veces	*sometimes*
		algunas veces	*sometimes*
nadie	*nobody, not anybody*	**alguien**	*somebody, someone*
		todo el mundo	*everybody*
nada	*nothing, not anything*	**algo**	*something*
		todo	*everything*

ningún,[1]	none, not any	algún,[1]	some
ninguno (-s),		alguno (-s),	
ninguna (-s)		alguna (-s)	
tampoco,	neither, not either	también	also
ni . . . tampoco			
todavía no	not yet	ya	already
ya no	not anymore	todavía	still
ni . . . ni	neither . . . nor	o . . . o	either . . . or

A. A negative word may be placed before the verb, in which case **no** is not used.

Nunca la veo.   *I never see her (it, you).*
Nadie quiere ir a su fiesta.   *Nobody wants to go to her party.*
Nadie le interesa.   *He (she) isn't interested in anybody.*
                                         You aren't interested in anybody.

B. A negative word may follow the verb, in which case **no** precedes the verb.

No sé **nada** de música.   *I don't know anything about music.*
No conocemos **a nadie** aquí.   *We don't know anybody here.*
No irán **tampoco**.   *They won't go either.*
No me escribió **ninguno**   *None of you wrote to me.*
    de ustedes.

C. Two or more negative words may be used at one time. They do not make the sentence affirmative, as two negatives do in English. **Nunca** is usually placed first.

Nunca lo he mencionado **a nadie**.
I have never mentioned it to anyone.

Nunca pido **nada a nadie**.
I never ask anything from anybody.

No he visto **nunca a nadie tampoco**.
I have never seen anyone either.

D. In a comparative sentence, indefinites generally take the negative form. This does not make the sentence negative.

---

1. See *La apócope 5.*

Toca **mejor que nunca**.	*He (she) plays better than ever.*
	You play better than ever.
Ella sabe **más que nadie**.	*She knows more than anybody.*

E.   Negatives are used after **sin**.

Salió **sin nada de dinero**.	*He (she, you) left without any money.*
sin ninguna dificultad	*without any difficulty*

3.3   No . . . más que

The expression **no . . . más que** means *only*.

No me dieron **más que** consejos.
The only thing they gave me was advice.

No tengo **más que** problemas.
The only thing I have is problems.

3.4   Los prefijos negativos: **in-, des-, dis-** (Negative prefixes *un-, dis-*)

The prefix **in-** becomes **im-** before **p**.

incapaz   **in**calculable   **in**consciente   **im**prudente   **im**personal
desplacer   **des**armar   **des**aparecer   **des**cuento   **dis**gusto

4 Los adjetivos

In Spanish, as in English, there are various kinds of adjectives: qualifying, possessive, interrogative, demonstrative, numerical, and indefinite.

4.1 Los adjetivos calificativos (Qualifying adjectives)

A. An adjective agrees in gender and number with the noun or pronoun that it modifies.

un libro rojo	unos libros rojos
una flor roja	unas flores rojas

B. Feminine of adjectives

1. Adjectives ending in **-o** in the masculine change the **-o** to **-a** to form the feminine.

blanco	blanca	precioso	preciosa
magnífico	magnífica	feo	fea

2. Adjectives ending in **-or, -ón, -án, -ín** and adjectives of nationality ending in a consonant add **-a** to form the feminine.

defensor	defensora	conductor	conductora
pelón	pelona	chiquitín	chiquitina
holgazán	holgazana	portador	portadora
francés	francesa	español	española
japonés	japonesa	portugués	portuguesa

The following exceptions have the same form for both genders.

exterior	mayor	mejor
interior	menor	peor
superior	anterior	marrón
inferior	posterior	

3. All other adjectives have the same form for both the masculine and feminine.

fácil	**azul**	**triste**
difícil	**gris**	**senil**
vulgar	**capaz**	**belga**
optimista	**hipócrita**	**israelita**
idealista	**socialista**	**comunista**

C. Plural of adjectives

1. Adjectives ending in a vowel add -s to form the plural.

rojo	**rojos**	moderno	**modernos**	amable	**amables**
roja	**rojas**	moderna	**modernas**	grande	**grandes**

2. Adjectives ending in a consonant add -es to form the plural.

feliz	**felices**	andaluz	**andaluces**	veloz	**veloces**

3. If an adjective modifies two or more nouns, one of which is masculine, the masculine plural form is used.

Juan, su madre, su tía, su hermana y su prima son **pequeños**.

D. Position of adjectives

1. In Spanish, an adjective usually follows the noun it modifies.

una silla **cómoda**	un hombre **simpático**	un vino **rojo**
una mesa **redonda**	un estudio **analítico**	un autor **famoso**

2. Some common adjectives denoting inherent characteristics such as **viejo, joven, pequeño, grande, bueno, malo, bonito,** and **hermoso** often precede the noun, although they may follow it.

un viejo **mueble**   una **buena** contestación   una **mala** costumbre
una **hermosa** mujer   un **pequeño** obstáculo   un **bonito** coche

3. When two or more adjectives modify one noun, one may precede the noun (such as **viejo** or **grande**), while the others follow the noun, separated by comas or joined by **y**.

un **viejo** castillo **moro**   un **bonito** vestido **rojo**
una mujer **alta, rubia, encantadora y rica**
un vestido **nuevo y caro**

4. If one of the adjectives is associated with the noun almost as a single concept, the conjunction **y** is not used.

un **famoso** autor **francés**   una **preciosa** catedral **gótica**

E.   A few adjectives have two different meanings depending upon whether
     they precede or follow the noun.

un **gran** hombre	*a great man*
un hombre **grande**	*a tall man*
¡**Pobre** mujer!	*Poor woman!*
una mujer **pobre**	*a moneyless woman, a poor woman*
una **sola** muchacha	*only one girl*
una muchacha **sola**	*a lonely girl, a girl alone*
Viven en la **misma** calle.	*They live on the same street.*
la calle **misma** del accidente	*the very street of the accident*
un amigo **viejo**	*an elderly friend*
un **viejo** amigo	*a long-standing friend*
una **verdadera** catástrofe	*a real catastrophe*
una historia **verdadera**	*a true story*
cierta promesa	*some promise*
una promesa **cierta**	*a sure promise*
un **antiguo** alumno	*an old student, a former student*
la historia **antigua**	*ancient history*
un coche **nuevo**	*a new car (brand-new)*
un **nuevo** coche	*a different car*

F.   In Spanish, an adjective may be used as a noun when it refers to a
     person or persons.

un **ciego**	*a blind man*
una **rubia**	*a blond woman*
unos **locos**	*some crazy people*
un **viejo**	*an old man*
los **muertos**	*the dead ones*
los **ricos**	*the rich people*
los **pobres**	*the poor people*
los **jóvenes**	*the young people*

G.   With the neuter article **lo**, the masculine form of the adjective functions
     as an abstract noun.

Lo difícil es perseverar.
The difficulty is to persevere.

Lo malo es que no tengo dinero.
The trouble is that I don't have any money.

Lo mejor perjudica **lo bueno**.
The best is detrimental to what is good.

Lo poco basta y **lo mucho** cansa.
A little is enough and too much is tiring.

4.2 Los adjetivos posesivos (Possessive adjectives)

A.   Unstressed forms

    1.   In Spanish, possessive adjectives agree in gender and number with the possessed object. The person is determined by the possessor. **Mi, tu,** and **su** have the same forms for both genders. The unstressed forms precede the noun.

yo tengo	**mi** libro	**mis** libros
	mi pluma	**mis** plumas
tú tienes	**tu** libro	**tus** libros
	tu pluma	**tus** plumas
él tiene	**su** libro	**sus** libros
	su pluma	**sus** plumas
ella tiene	**su** libro	**sus** libros
	su pluma	**sus** plumas
usted tiene	**su** libro	**sus** libros
	su pluma	**sus** plumas
nosotros tenemos	**nuestro** libro	**nuestros** libros
	nuestra pluma	**nuestras** plumas
vosotros tenéis	**vuestro** libro	**vuestros** libros
	vuestra pluma	**vuestras** plumas
ellos tienen	**su** libro	**sus** libros
	sus pluma	**sus** plumas
ellas tienen	**su** libro	**sus** libros
	su pluma	**sus** plumas
ustedes tienen	**su** libro	**sus** libros
	su pluma	**sus** plumas

    2.   Since **su** and **sus** have several meanings, they may be replaced for clarity by the article + noun + **de él, de ella, de ellos, de ellas, de usted,** or **de ustedes.**

su amigo:	el amigo de él	*his friend*
	el amigo de ella	*her friend*
	el amigo de usted	*your friend*
	el amigo de ellos	*their friend*
	el amigo de ellas	*their friend*
	el amigo de ustedes	*your friend*
sus amigos:	los amigos de él	*his friends*
	los amigos de ella	*her friends*
	los amigos de usted	*your friends*
	los amigos de ellos	*their friends*
	los amigos de ellas	*their friends*
	los amigos de ustedes	*your friends*

B.   Stressed forms

The stressed forms of possessive adjectives are used in direct address, after the verb **ser,** or to express the English *of mine, of yours,* and so on. The stressed forms follow the nouns.

mío	**mía**	**míos**	**mías**
tuyo	**tuya**	**tuyos**	**tuyas**
suyo	**suya**	**suyos**	**suyas**
nuestro	**nuestra**	**nuestros**	**nuestras**
vuestro	**vuestra**	**vuestros**	**vuestras**
suyo	**suya**	**suyos**	**suyas**

Cálmate, **hija mía.**	*Calm down, daughter (of mine).*
¡Dios mío!	*My God!*
Es una **amiga nuestra.**	*She is a friend of ours.*
El reloj de oro es **mío.**	*The gold watch is mine.*
Éstas son **tuyas,** no **mías.**	*These are yours, not mine.*

4.3 Los adjetivos interrogativos (Interrogative adjectives)

The interrogative adjective is placed before the noun and has a written accent.

¿qué?	*what?*
¿cuánto?	*how much?*
¿cuántos? , **¿cuántas?**	*how many?*

¿Qué hora es?	**¿Cuántas** lenguas aprenden?
¿Cuánto dinero quieres?	**¿En qué** calle vive usted?

4.4 Los adjetivos demostrativos (Demonstrative adjectives)

Demonstrative adjectives point out objects. They vary according to the gender and number of the objects they modify and according to the distance in space, time, or thought between the objects and the speaker. Demonstrative adjectives are repeated before each noun they modify.

este lápiz	*this pencil*	esta pluma	*this pen (near)*
ese lápiz	*that pencil*	esa pluma	*that pen (far away)*
aquel lápiz	*that pencil*	aquella pluma	*that pen (further away)*
estos lápices	*these pencils*	estas plumas	*these pens (near)*
esos lápices	*those pencils*	esas plumas	*those pens (far away)*
aquellos lápices	*those pencils*	aquellas plumas	*those pens (further away)*

Este libro, esa pluma y aquel lápiz son míos.
This book, that pen, and that pencil (over there) are mine.

4.5 Los adjetivos numerales (Numerical adjectives)

A. Cardinal numbers

0	cero	22	veintidós (veinte y dos)
1	un(o), una	23	veintitrés (veinte y tres)
2	dos	24	veinticuatro (veinte y cuatro)
3	tres	25	veinticinco (veinte y cinco)
4	cuatro	26	veintiséis (veinte y seis)
5	cinco	27	veintisiete (veinte y siete)
6	seis	28	veintiocho (veinte y ocho)
7	siete	29	veintinueve (veinte y nueve)
8	ocho	30	treinta
9	nueve	31	treinta y un(o), -a
10	diez	32	treinta y dos
11	once	40	cuarenta
12	doce	41	cuarenta y un(o), -a
13	trece	42	cuarenta y dos
14	catorce	50	cincuenta
15	quince	51	cincuenta y un(o), -a
16	dieciséis (diez y seis)	52	cincuenta y dos
17	diecisiete (diez y siete)	60	sesenta
18	dieciocho (diez y ocho)	61	sesenta y un(o), -a
19	diecinueve (diez y nueve)	62	sesenta y dos
20	veinte	70	setenta
21	veintiunó, -a (veinte y uno, -a)	71	setenta y un(o), -a

72	setenta y dos	600	seiscientos, -as
80	ochenta	700	setecientos, -as
81	ochenta y un(o), -a	800	ochocientos, -as
82	ochenta y dos	900	novecientos, -as
90	noventa	1.000	mil
91	noventa y un(o), -a	1.001	mil un(o), -a
92	noventa y dos	1.002	mil dos
100	cien, ciento	1.100	mil cien
101	ciento un(o), -a	1.500	mil quinientos, -as
102	ciento dos	2.000	dos mil
200	doscientos, doscientas	2.001	dos mil un(o), -a
201	doscientos un(o), -a	10.000	diez mil
202	doscientos dos	100.000	cien mil
300	trescientos, trescientas	1.000.000	un millón (de)
400	cuatrocientos, -as	2.000.000	dos millones (de)
500	quinientos, -as	1.000.000.000	mil millones

1.   Centuries are indicated by cardinal numbers.

el siglo veinte   *the twentieth century*
el siglo nueve   *the ninth century*

2.   The **-o** of **uno** is dropped before masculine nouns.

Es un edificio muy alto.

3.   **Veintiuno** becomes **veintiún** before masculine nouns.

El profesor tiene **veintiún alumnos** en la clase.

4.   **Cien** is used before nouns and before **mil** and **millons**. (See also
     La apócope 5.)

Pocos hombres viven más de **cien años**.

B.   Ordinal numbers

1st	**primer(o), -a**	10th	**décimo, -a**
2nd	**segundo, -a**	11th	**undécimo, -a**
3rd	**tercer(o), -a**	12th	**duodécimo, -a**
4th	**cuarto, -a**	13th	**decimotercio, -a**
5th	**quinto, -a**	14th	**decimocuarto, -a**
6th	**sexto, -a**	15th	**decimoquinto, -a**
7th	**séptimo, -a**	16th	**decimosexto, -a**
8th	**octavo, -a**	17th	**decimoséptimo, -a**
9th	**noveno, -a**	18th	**decimoctavo, -a**

19th	decimonono, -a	1,000th	milésimo, -a
20th	vigésimo, -a	1,000,000th	millonésimo, -a
100th	centésimo, -a		

1. Above **décimo**, the cardinal numbers are generally used. They follow the noun.

    la calle Diez y Ocho

2. Ordinal numbers precede the noun they modify except in titles of rulers and popes.

    Felipe **Segundo**   Carlos **Quinto**   Paulo **Sexto**   Juan **Veintitrés**

3. **Primero** and **tercero** drop the -o before masculine singular nouns.

    el **primer** lugar   el **tercer** día

4. The article is used with an ordinal number. Both agree in gender and in number with the noun they modify.

    Te lo repito por **la tercera vez.**

5. The only ordinal number used in dates is **primero**. Cardinal numbers are used otherwise.

    el **primero** de septiembre   el **once** de junio

C. Fractions

1/2	**medio, -a** or **la mitad de . . .**
1/3	**un tercio,** or **la tercera parte de . . .**
1/4	**un cuarto,** or **la cuarta parte de . . .**
2/3	**dos tercios**
3/4	**tres cuartos**
7/10	**siete décimos**

Through **décimo**, ordinal numbers are used except for **medio** and **tercio**. Above **décimo**, **-avo** is usually added to the cardinal number, though some other forms exist.

2/50 **dos cincuentavos**   7/20 **siete veintavos, siete vigésimos**

4.6 Los adjetivos indefinidos (Indefinite adjectives)

Indefinite adjectives are also used as indefinite pronouns. (See also *Los pronombres indefinidos y negativos 18.5.*)

A.   **Cada** (*each*) is used only before a singular noun. It is invariable.

    Cada opinión tiene su valor.
    Me interrumpe a **cada** momento.

B.   **algún, alguna, algunos, algunas** (*some, a few*)

    Tendrá **algún** propósito.   **Algunas** plantas no crecen rápidamente.

C.   **varios, varias** (*several, various*)

    Conozco **varios** países.   **Varias** respuestas son posibles.
    Le escribieron **varias** veces.   **Varias** personalidades atendieron.

D.   **ningún, ninguna, ningunos, ningunas** (*no*) (See also *Las palabras negativas y afirmativas 3.2.*)

    Ningún trabajo le gusta.   **Ninguna** explicación me dio.

E.   **unos, unas** (*some*)

    Ayer escribí a **unos** amigos. Quiero hacer **unas** preguntas.

F.   **otro, otra, otros, otras** (*other, another*)

    en **otra** ocasión   con **otras** palabras   Tengo **otro** hermano.

G.   **cierto, cierta, ciertos, ciertas** (*some, certain*)

    Ciertos profesores son injustos.
    Ciertas preguntas son fáciles.

    When placed after the noun, **cierto** is a qualifying adjective meaning *sure*.

    Es una victoria **cierta**.

H.   **todo, toda, todos, todas** (*all, each, every, the entire*)

    El profesor nos explicó **toda** la lección.
    The professor explained the entire lesson to us.

    Todo trabajo merece salario.
    All (any) work deserves a salary.

    Todos los hombres son mortales.
    All men are mortal.

todos los días
every day

Idiom: **todo** el mundo   *everybody*

I.   **tal, tales** (*such*)

Nunca he visto **tal** espectáculo.
en **tales** circunstancias   de **tal** manera   por **tal** motivo

J.   **cualquier, cualquiera, cualesquiera** (*any, just any, whatever*)

Before a noun, only the form **cualquier** may be used. After a noun,
only **cualquiera** may be used.

en **cualquier** momento y **cualquier** hora
un día **cualquiera**
Miguel de Unamuno no es un autor **cualquiera.**

5 La apócope

A. Some adjectives lose the final -o when they precede a masculine singular noun.

uno	un día solamente
bueno	un buen amigo
malo	está de mal humor
alguno	en algún sitio
ninguno	de ningún modo
primero	el primer día de la semana
tercero	el tercer piso
postrero	el postrer suspiro

B. Grande becomes gran before any singular noun. In this position it means *great*.

un gran poeta   una gran obra de arte

C. Ciento becomes cien before nouns and before mil and millones. It is not shortened before any other numerals.

Este autor escribió más de cien libros.
Es una ciudad de cien mil habitantes.
Este autor escribió más de ciento cincuenta libros.

D. Santo becomes San before masculine names, except for those which begin with Do- or To-.

San Pedro   San Pablo   Santo Domingo   Santo Tomás   Santa María

E. Cualquiera becomes cualquier when it precedes a noun.

Cualquier día   cualquier semana

6 Los adverbios

The adverb is invariable and, as its name indicates, usually modifies a verb. It is also used occasionally to modify an adjective or another adverb.

6.1 La formación de los adverbios (Formation of adverbs)

A. Adverbs of manner answer the question *how?* Most are formed by adding **-mente** to the feminine singular form of the adjective.

lento	**lentamente**	claro	**claramente**
precioso	**preciosamente**	rápido	**rápidamente**
frío	**fríamente**	fácil	**fácilmente**
triste	**tristemente**	natural	**naturalmente**
vulgar	**vulgarmente**	anterior	**anteriormente**

B. When two or more adverbs ending in **-mente** are used consecutively, the ending is used only on the last adverb. The others remain in the feminine form of the adjective.

Hablan **clara, lenta e inteligentemente.**

C. When the adjective has an accent, it is retained in the adverb.

rápido   **rápidamente**   fácil   **fácilmente**   cortés   **cortésmente**

D. In Spanish, prepositional phrases are frequently used instead of adverbs in **-mente.**

frecuentemente	**con frecuencia**	violentamente	**con violencia**
regularmente	**por lo regular**	calmadamente	**con calma**

E. Many words may be used either as adjectives or as adverbs. As adjectives, they **vary** in gender and number; as adverbs, they are invariable.

Tengo **muchos** problemas.   Comemos **mucho.**
Hay **demasiados** alumnos en esta clase que fuman **demasiado.**

[21]

F.   Some adverbs have a different form than their corresponding adjectives.

bueno, **bien**   malo, **mal**   tanto, **tan** (or **tanto**)

G.   **Recientemente** becomes **recién** before a past participle used as an adjective.

Los **recién** casados no vinieron.   Es un **recién** llegado.

H.   Adverbs may express

TIME: ayer, antes, después, tarde, temprano, nunca,
             jamás, aún, ya, ahora, cuando, ¿cuándo?, hoy,
             manaña, anoche, todavía, mientras
PLACE: aquí, ahí, allí, acá, allá, cerca, lejos,
             debajo, abajo, arriba, dentro, adentro, fuera,
             dondequiera, donde, ¿dónde? , ¿adónde?
MANNER: bien, como, ¿cómo?, mal, apenas, según,
             medio, aprisa, mejor, peor, despacio,
             recio, así, and all adverbs in -mente
QUANTITY: mucho, poco, bastante, muy, tan, tanto, cuanto,
             ¿cuánto?

6.2   La posición de los adverbios (Position of adverbs)

A.   Although there are no strict rules, the adverb is usually placed after the verb it modifies.

Sus amigos beben **mucho**.   El tiempo pasó **rápidamente**.

B.   The adverb is also placed before the adjective or adverb it modifies and after the noun.

Sus ideas son **muy** buenas.
Alicia se levanta **muy** tarde.
Es una tarea **extremadamente** difícil.

C.   An adverb placed at the beginning of a sentence is usually more emphatic.

Nunca va a la iglesia.
Tanto se lo pedí que por fin lo hizo.

D.   The adverbs **más que, menos que, mejor que, peor que, tanto como, tan ... como**, and expressions such as **más de . . ., menos de . . .** are used in comparisons. (See *El comparativo 8.*)

Las expresiones de
7 cantidad

No article is used between the preposition **de** and the noun that follows in expressions of quantity.

una taza de café	*a cup of coffee*
una gota de agua	*a drop of water*
un puñado de arena	*a handfull of sand*
un ramo de flores	*a bunch of flowers*
una docena de huevos	*a dozen eggs*
una colección de sellos	*a stamp collection*
una decena de personas	*around ten people*
una rebanada de pan	*a slice of bread*
una tajada de carne	*a slice of meat*
un pedazo de pastel	*a piece of cake*
un montón de documentos	*a pile of documents*
una copa de vino	*a glass of wine*
una botella de cerveza	*a bottle of beer*
una serie de acontecimientos	*series of events*
una libra de mantequilla	*a pound of butter*
una lata de sardinas	*a can of sardines*
una caja de dulces	*a box of candy*
una hilera de árboles	*a row of trees*

By adding **-ena** to certain cardinal numbers, expressions of quantity are formed which convey the idea of approximate numbers.

una decena de . . .	*around ten . . .*
una quincena de . . .	*around fifteen . . .*
una veintena de . . .	*around twenty . . .*
una treintena de . . .	*around thirty . . .*
una cuarentena de . . .	*around forty . . .*
una cincuentena de . . .	*around fifty . . .*
una centena de . . .	*around a hundred . . .*
un centenar de . . .	*around a hundred . . .*

[23]

Una docena de is used as a definite measure.

una docena de . . .	*a dozen* . . .

The idea of **around** or **about** can also be expressed by **unos +** a cardinal number.

unos ocho	*about eight*
unos veinte	*about twenty*
unos ochenta	*about eighty*

8 El comparativo

A.   **Más ... que** (*more ... than*), **menos ... que** (*less ... than*), **tanto, -a ... como** (*as much ... as*), and **tantos, -as ... como** (*as many ... as*) are used to compare nouns.

COMPARISON OF SUPERIORITY	**más**	} + noun + {	**que**
COMPARISON OF INFERIORITY	**menos**		**que**
COMPARISON OF EQUALITY	**tanto(s), -a(s)**		**como**

Juana tiene **más amigos que** Alicia.
Roberto tiene **menos dinero que** Pablo.
Mi hermano tiene **tantos trajes como** yo.

B.   **Más ... que, menos ... que, tan ... como** (*as ... as*) are used to compare adjectives or adverbs. **Tan** is not used before **mucho.**

COMPARISON OF SUPERIORITY	**más**		adjective	**que**
COMPARISON OF INFERIORITY	**menos**	} +	or	+ { **que**
COMPARISON OF EQUALITY	**tan**		adverb	**como**

Alicia es **más bonita que** María.
Alice is prettier than Maria.

Mi trabajo es **menos interesante que** el tuyo.
My work is less interesting than yours.

Mi madre es **tan alta como** mi padre.
My mother is as tall as my father.

C.   **Tanto como** (*as much as*), because it is an adverb, is invariable.

Trabajo **tanto como** tú.   No duermo **tanto como** quisiera.

D.   Before a number **de** is used instead of **que.**

Es un viaje que dura **menos de cinco** horas.
Él pagó **más de veinte** dólares por la cena.

E. In a comparison of nouns involving two clauses, the second clause is intro-
    duced by **del que, de los que, de la que,** or **de las que.**

Compré más comida **de la que** necesitaba.
I bought more food than (that which) I needed.

Roberto tiene más hijos **de los que** puede mantener.
Robert has more children than (those whom) he can support.

F. In a comparison involving two clauses, the second clause is introduced by **de
    lo que** if an adjective, an adverb, or a whole idea is being compared.

Entiendo más **de lo que** usted cree.
I understand more than (what) you think. (what = whole idea)

Este empleado es más inteligente **de lo que** esperábamos.
This employee is more intelligent than (what) we expected.

Trabajas peor **de lo que** me habían dicho.
You work worse than (what) I was told.

G. In a comparison, the adjectives **superior** and **inferior** are followed by the
    preposition **a.**

Su idea es **superior a** la mía.
Esta cualidad es **inferior a** la que usted me ofreció.

H. The comparatives **más, menos,** and **tan** are repeated before each adjective or
    adverb.

Tu coche es **más caro, menos rápido** y **menos cómodo que** el mío.
Your car is more expensive and less fast and comfortable than mine.

Esta casa es **tan grande, tan moderna** y **tan bonita como** la mía.
This house is as big, modern, and pretty as mine.

I. Irregular comparatives

ADJECTIVES		ADVERBS		COMPARATIVES	
mucho(s), -a(s)	*much, many*	**mucho**	*much*	**más**	*more*
poco(s), -a(s)	*little, few*	**poco**	*little*	**menos**	*fewer, less*
bueno(s), -a(s)	*good*	**bien**	*well*	**mejor**	*better*
malo(s), -a(s)	*bad*	**mal**	*badly*	**peor**	*worse*
grande(s)	*large*			**mayor**	*older, larger*
pequeño(s), -a(s)	*small*			**menor**	*younger, smaller*

1.   The irregular comparatives of the adjectives are used for both genders and agree in number with the nouns they modify.

2.   The plural forms are **mejores, peores, mayores, menores. Más** and **menos** are invariable.

3.   **Grande** and **pequeño** may also be compared in the regular manner. Usually **más grande** and **más pequeño** refer to size, whereas **mayor** and **menor** refer to age.

Yo soy **más pequeño que** mi hermano pero él es **mayor que** yo.
I am smaller than my brother but he is older than I.

Las composiciones de Juan son **mejores que** las de Jorge.
Juan's compositions are better than Jorge's.

4.   Adverbs are invariable.

Es **mejor** prevenir que lamentar.   *Prevention is better than lament.*
Han trabajado **peor** que ustedes.   *They worked worse than you.*

J.   The expression **no . . . más que** means *only.* (See *La negación 3.3.*)

9 El superlativo

9.1 El superlativo de los adjetivos (Superlative of adjectives)

A. There are two kinds of superlatives: superiority and inferiority. They are formed by placing **el, la, los,** or **las** before **más** or **menos** + an adjective.

María es **la más inteligente.**
María is the most intelligent.

Sus contestaciones son **las más largas.**
His (her, your, their) answers are the longest.

Este libro es **el menos interesante.**
This book is the least interesting one.

B. When a complement follows, it is introduced by **de.**

María es la más inteligente **de** la clase.
María is the most intelligent one in the class.

Sus contestaciones son las más largas **de** todas.
His (her, your, their) answers are the longest of all.

Este libro es el menos interesante **de** la biblioteca.
This book is the least interesting one in the library.

C. Irregular superlative of adjectives

el mejor		el peor	
la mejor	*the best*	la peor	*the worst*
los mejores		los peores	
las mejores		las peores	

el mayor		el menor	
la mayor	*the oldest,*	la menor	*the youngest,*
los mayores	*the largest*	los menores	*the smallest*
las mayores		las menores	

[28]

Este vino es **el mejor.**
This wine is the best.

Teresa es **la mejor** estudiante.
Teresa is the best student.

Estas películas son **las peores** que he visto.
These movies are the worst ones I have seen.

Rosa es **la mayor** de las hermanas.
Rosa is the oldest of the sisters.

D. The definite article is not used after a possessive adjective.

Perdí a mi mejor amigo.
Sus más grandes esfuerzos fueron inútiles.
mi más querida hermana *or* **mi hermana más querida**

E. Some adjectives have two forms in the comparative and superlative.

malo	**más malo**	**el más malo**
	peor	**el peor**
pequeño	**más pequeño**	**el más pequeño**
	menor	**el menor**
joven	**más joven**	**el más joven**
	menor	**el menor**
grande	**más grande**	**el más grande**
	mayor	**el mayor**
viejo	**más viejo**	**el más viejo**
	mayor	**el mayor**

9.2 El superlativo de los adverbios (Superlative of adverbs)

The comparative and superlative forms of adverbs are the same. The article is not used in the superlative.

Caruso cantaba **mejor que** nadie.
Caruso used to sing better than anyone.

Pepe es el que **peor** toca la guitarra.
Pepe is the one who plays the guitar the worst.

Mayor and **menor** are not used as adverbs.

9.3 Algunas expresiones adverbiales (Some adverbial expressions)

A. **cada vez más** (*more and more*), **cada vez menos** (*less and less*)

Este estudiante llega **cada vez más tarde**.
This student arrives later each time.

Este curso se vuelve **cada vez menos intersante**.
This course becomes less and less interesting.

B. **cuanto más** + verb . . . **tanto más** + verb (*the more* + verb . . . *the more* + verb)

Cuanto más come, tanto más engorda.
The more you eat, the fatter you get.

Cuanto menos leo, tanto menos aprendo.
The less I read, the less I learn.

Cuanto más ahorro, tanto menos gasto.
The more I save, the less I spend.

C. **de mal en peor** (*from bad to worse*)

La situación económica va **de mal en peor**.
The economic conditions are going from bad to worse.

9.4 El superlativo absoluto (Absolute superlative)

A. The absolute superlative expresses a very high degree. It is formed (1) by placing **muy** before an adjective or adverb, or (2) by adding the suffix **-ísimo** (**-ísima, -ísimos, -ísimas**) to an adjective, and **-ísimamente** to an adverb, dropping first the final vowel of the adjective.

| alto | { **muy alto** / **altísimo** | raro | { **muy raro** / **rarísimo** | malo | { **muy malo** / **malísimo** |

| rápidamente | { **muy rápidamente** / **rapidísimamente** | fácilmente | { **muy fácilmente** / **facilísimamente** |

B. Adjectives ending in **-co, -go, -z,** or **-ble** change these letters to **-qu, -gu, -c, -bil** respectively before adding **-ísimo**.

| rico | **riquísimo** | feliz | **felicísimo** |
| largo | **larguísimo** | amable | **amabilísimo** |

10 Las preposiciones

Prepositions are invariable and show the relationship between two words in a sentence. After a preposition, a verb in Spanish is normally in the infinitive form.

Exception: según

según dice la ley   *according to what the law says*

10.1 Las preposiciones principales (Principal prepositions)

a	*to, at, in*	**hacia**	*towards*
ante	*before, in front of*	**hasta**	*till, until*
bajo	*under*	**para**	*for, in order to*
con	*with*	**por**	*by, through, per, for*
contra	*against*	**salvo**	*except*
de	*of, from*	**según**	*according to*
desde	*since*	**sin**	*without*
durante	*during*	**sobre**	*on, upon*
en	*in*	**tras**	*after*
entre	*between, among*		

10.2 Las principales frases preposicionales (Principal propositional phrases)

a causa de	*on account of*
acerca de	*about*
además de	*besides*
a diferencia de	*unlike*
a excepción de	*with the exception of*
a la derecha de	*to the right of*
a la izquierda de	*to the left of*
al cabo de	*at the end of*
al exterior de	*on the outside of*

al final de	*at the end of*
al lado de	*beside, next to*
a lo largo de	*alongside*
al pie de	*at the foot of*
alrededor de	*around*
antes de	*before* (time)
a pesar de	*in spite of*
a propósito de	*with regard to*
a través de	*across, through*
cerca de	*near*
delante de	*before* (space)
dentro de	*within*
después de	*after* (time)
detrás de	*behind*
encima de	*on top of, above*
en cuanto a	*as for, as to*
en frente de	*opposite, facing*
en lugar de	*instead of*
en medio de	*in the middle of*
en vez de	*instead of*
frente a	*opposite, facing*
fuera de	*outside*
gracias a	*thanks to*
junto a	*next to*
lejos de	*far from*
más allá de	*beyond*
por causa de	*on account of, owing to*
por encima de	*above*
por medio de	*by means of*

(See also *Los modismos con las preposiciones 11.*)

10.3 Los usos de las preposiciones **a, de, por, para** (Uses of prepositions)

A. The usual meaning of **a** is *to* or *at*.

1. The preposition **a** is used before a direct object when the object refers to a specific person or a personified object.

Encontré **a mi hermano** en el cine.
I found my brother at the movies.

Temo **a la muerte.**
I fear Death.

Visitamos **a los Kennedy** la semana pasada.
We visited the Kennedys last week.

Vio **a María** todos los días.
He (she, you) saw María every day.

The preposition **a** is also used when the direct object is the relative pronoun **quien(es)**; the interrogative pronoun **¿quién(es)?** ; or the indefinite pronouns **alguien, nadie, alguno (-a, -os, -as)**, or **ninguno (-a, -os, -as)**, when these refer to persons.

¿A quién llamó usted?
Whom did you call?

No hemos visto **a nadie.**
We didn't see anyone.

Están esperando **a algunos amigos franceses.**
They are expecting some French friends.

The preposition **a** is not used unless the noun refers to a specific person, after the verb **tener**, and with the verb **querer** when it means *to want.*

Estoy buscando **un empleado.**
Tengo **un hermano médico.**
Queremos **el jefe** ahora mismo.

But: Quiero **a mis padres.**

2. The preposition **a** is used with the indirect object.

Daremos todas las muñecas **a la niña.**
El profesor tiene que enseñar la gramática **a los estudiantes.**
Escribí **al director** de la compañía.

3. **A** is used with the verb **ir** + an infinitive to form the near future. (See also *El futuro cercano 36.3.*)

Van a estudiar toda la noche.
They are going to study all night.

Vamos a salir antes de las ocho.
We are going to go out before eight o'clock.

4.   **A** is placed before nouns, pronouns, and infinitives when they follow verbs of motion. (See also *Los verbos usados con a 43.4.*)

Este verano **iremos a Cádiz.**
Luis **se acercó a la puerta.**
Luis **se acercó a ella** (la puerta).
Vamos a ver.
Subimos al tren.

5.   **A** is used to express the time an action takes place.

Me levanto **a las siete** de la mañana.
Por lo general cenamos **a las ocho.**
Darán este programa **a las tres** de la tarde.
Los felicité **al final** del concierto.
Empezó a llover **al amanecer.**

6.   **A** is used in many common expressions which do not have exact English equivalents.

a menudo	*often*
a la hora	*on time*
a tiempo	*in time*
hecho a mano	*handmade*
Mi coche está **a la mano.**	*My car is on hand.*
mano a mano	*equal match, on equal terms*

El partido de ajedrez resultó en **un mano a mano** interesante.
The chess game turned out to be an interesting equal match.

(See also *Los modismos con las preposiciones 11.*)

B.   The usual meaning of **de** is *from* or *of*. (See also *Los verbos usados con de 43.5.*)

1.   **De** denotes possession: **El coche de Juan** es nuevo.
                                     Juan's car is new.

     authorship: **un poema de García Lorca**
                    a poem by García Lorca

     origin: Es **de Guatemala.**
                He (she) is from Guatemala.

     cause: Se muere **de sed.**
               He (she) is dying from thirst.

2.   **De** between two nouns denotes material or purpose.

una mesa de marmol	*a marble table*
una máquina de escribir	*a typewriter*
un cuarto de baño	*a bathroom*
una cortina de hierro	*an iron curtain*
un cepillo de dientes	*a toothbrush*
una clase de música	*a music class*
un número de teléfono	*a telephone number*
una agencia de viaje	*a travel agency*
un viaje de placer	*a pleasure trip*
una sala de espera	*a waiting room*

3. **De** is used in expressions of quantity. (See also *Las expresiones de cantidad 7.*)

    una taza de café   **una docena de huevos**

4. **De** is used in many common expressions which do not have exact English equivalents.

estar de luto	*to be in mourning*
vestido de blanco	*dressed in white*
de la parte de	*in behalf of*
de nada	*you are welcome*
de nuevo	*again*
de prisa	*rapidly*

(See also *Los modismos con las preposiciones 11.*)

C. The usual meaning of **por** is *by, through, per,* or *for.*

1. The preposition **por** introduces the agent by whom an action is performed. (See also *La voz pasiva 46.*)

    Esta obra fue realizada **por un autor español.**
    Constantinopla fue tomada **por los cruzados** en 1204.
    El examen será corregido **por el profesor.**

2. **Por** expresses the duration of an action and is used in indefinite time expressions.

    He vivido en Colombia **por dos años.**
    Me ausentaré **por una semana.**
    Manuela enseña **por la noche.** (*or* Manuela enseña en la noche.)
    Vamos al mercado **por la mañana.** (*or* Vamos al mercado en la mañana.)
    But: Vamos al mercado a las ocho **de la manaña.**

3. **Por** is used with the object of an errand after verbs such as **ir,
    venir, mandar, enviar, volver,** and **regresar.**

    Fueron por la cerveza.
    Tienen que **volver por** sus libros.
    Mandó por un médico.

4. **Por** is used to express the English *in exchange for.*

    Vendí mi coche **por quinientos dólares.**
    Quiero cambiar mi coche **por uno nuevo.**

5. **Por** expresses the English *through, along,* or *by* after a verb of
    motion.

    Entraron **por la cocina.**
    Me entra **por un oído** y me sale **por el otro.**
    Nos paseamos **por el parque.**
    Caminó **por la orilla** del río.

6. **Por** is used to express a reason or motive.

    No se casó **por amor** sino **por dinero.**
    No como mucho **por no engordarme.**
    Pinto **por afición** al arte.

7. **Por** is used to indicate manner or means.

    El correo llegó **por avión.**
    Transmitieron el programa **por satélite.**

8. With persons, **por** is used to express opinion, concept, or belief.

    Este hombre pasa **por rico.**
    La dejaron **por muerta.**
    Se le tiene **por caballero.**
    Le arrestaron **por borracho.**

9. **Por** is used to express the English *per* or *by the.*

    Mi agente cobra el diez **por ciento.**
    Este avión vuela a novecientos kilómetros **por hora.**
    Los huevos se venden **por docenas.**
    Van al colegio cinco veces **por semana.**

10. **Por** expresses the English *times* in a multiplication.

    Dos por tres son seis.
    Ocho por nueve son setenta y dos.

11.   **Por** is used to express the English *in behalf of, for the sake of, in place of,* or *in favor of.*

Votaré **por el candidato** demócrata.
Contestaré **por mi madre.**
Lo hice **por tu hermano.**
¡Por Dios!

12.   **Estar por** + infinitive expresses the English *to remain to be* + verb.

Todo está aún **por hacer.**
Everything remains to be done yet.

El contrato **está por ratificarse.**
The contract remains to be ratified.

Todo eso **está por verse.**
All that remains to be seen.

13.   After verbs of movement, **por** may be used with other prepositions.

Se escapó **por detrás de** los coches.
He escaped (going along) behind the cars.

14.   **Por** is used in many common expressions which have no exact English equivalents.

por ahora	*for the present*
por cierto	*indeed*
¿por dónde?	*which way?*
por encima	*slightly, superficially, over*
por eso	*that is why*
por favor	*please*
por fin	*finally*
por lo menos	*at least*
por lo tanto	*therefore*
por lo visto	*apparently*
por si acaso	*if by chance*
por supuesto	*of course*

(See also *Los modismos con las preposiciones 11.*)

D.   The usual meaning of **para** is *in order to* or *for.*

1.   **Para** indicates a purpose.

Estudio **para médico.**

Mi padre me dio el dinero **para un coche nuevo**.

2. When used before an infinitive, **para** indicates purpose and expresses the English *in order to*.

Necesito papel **para escribir**.
Hay que trabajar **para vivir**.
Tenemos que estudiar mucho **para aprender**.

3. **Estar** + **para** + an infinitive indicates that an action is about to
happen.

Estamos para salir.
We are about (ready) to go out.

Estaban para ir de compras cuando empezó a llover.
They were about (ready) to go shopping when it started to rain.

4. **Para** indicates the special use or purpose of an object.

un cepillo para el pelo	*a hairbrush*
una taza para té	*a teacup*
una botella para vino	*a wine bottle*
una jaula para pájaros	*a bird cage*

5. **Para** is used to indicate destination or direction.

Tengo que salir **para Francia** mañana.
Compró un ramo de flores **para su esposa**.
Este paquete es **para ti**; el otro es **para el correo**.

6. **Para** is used to indicate a certain time, date, or deadline in the
future.

Tienen una cita **para el sábado**.
No hay que dejar **para mañana** lo que se puede hacer hoy.
Estaremos de regreso **para las diez**.

7. When comparing a person, object, or situation with others of its
kind, **para** expresses the English *for* or *considering (that)*.

Hace buen tiempo **para la estación**.
Para ser un hombre viejo, baila muy bien.
Esta mujer se ve muy bien **para su edad**.
Para ser extranjero, habla muy bien el español.

8. **Para con** is used to express behavior toward a person or persons.

Es ingrato **para con** sus padres.
He is ungrateful towards his parents.

9.   **Para** is used in common expressions which do not have exact English equivalents.

para colmo	*on top of everything*
No es para tanto.	*It is not that important.*

E.   Notes

1.   **para** vs. **por**

Para and **por** frequently mean *for* in English. Both have definite uses, however, and cannot be interchanged. Generally speaking **para** implies an objective, a purpose, or the destination of an action. **Por** implies a cause or a motive stimulating an action.

2.   The usual meaning of the preposition **en** is *in*.

en España   en buena salud   en el libro

Before an expression of time, **en** indicates the time required to do or accomplish something.

Hice el trabajo **en dos horas.**   Leí este libro **en una noche.**

En often has the meaning *on*.

en venta	*on sale*	**en el teléfono**	*on the phone*
en la mesa	*on the table*	**en la pared**	*on the wall*

(See also *Los modismos con las preposiciones 11*.)

3.   **Dentro de** is used to indicate future time or a spatial relationship. It expresses the English *within* or *in*.

Saldremos **dentro de dos días.**
Recibiré mi diploma **dentro de un año.**
El regalo está **dentro de la caja.**

10.4 Las contracciones del artículo definido y las preposiciones (Contractions of the definite article and prepositions)

A.   When the prepositions **de** or **a** precede the article **el**, they contract with it.

de + el = del	*of the*
a + el = al	*to the, at the*

B.   The pronouns **mí, ti**, and **sí** contract with the preposition **con** to form **conmigo, contigo**, and **consigo** respectively. (See also *Los pronombres 18.1D.*)

11 Los modismos con las preposiciones

For verbs using a preposition before an infinitive which follows see *El infinitivo 43.*

11.1 Los modismos con **a** (Idioms with **a**)

anterior a	*prior to*
atreverse a	*to dare*
gracias a	*thanks to*
inclinado a	*prone to*
junto a	*next to*
respecto a	*concerning, in regard to*
saber a	*to taste like*
ser aficionado a	*to be fond of*
tocante a	*concerning, in regard to*

11.2 Los modismos con **de** (Idioms with **de**)

aburrido de	*bored with*
acerca de	*regarding, about*
además de	*besides*
alrededor de	*around*
antes de	*before* (time)
aparte de	*besides*
asustado de	*afraid of*
cansado de	*tired of*
cargado de	*loaded with*
cerca de	*near*
contento de	*happy with*
cubierto de	*covered with*
darse cuenta de	*to realize that*
delante de	*before* (space)
dentro de	*within*

descontento de	*displeased with*
después de	*after* (time)
detrás de	*behind*
diferente de	*different from*
digno de	*worthy of*
enamorado de	*in love with*
encantado de	*pleased to*
es hora de	*it is time to*
estar a punto de	*to be about to*
fuera de	*outside*
harto de	*satiated with*
lejos de	*far from*
loco de	*very fond of*
lleno de	*full of*
muerto de	*very, extremely*
oír hablar de	*to hear about*
orgulloso de	*proud of*
satisfecho de	*satisfied with*
tener cara de	*to seem*
tener el derecho de	*to have the right to*
tener el propósito de	*to have in mind to, to plan*
tener ganas de	*to have a desire for, to feel like*
tener la culpa de	*to be to blame, to be at fault*
tener lástima de	*to feel sorry for*
tener miedo de (a)	*to fear*

11.3 Los modismos empezando por **a** (Idioms beginning with **a**)

a bordo	*on board*
a caballo	*on horseback*
a causa de	*on account of*
a ciegas	*blindly*
a compás	*in correct musical time*
a continuación	*then, following, as follows*
a costa de	*at the expense of*
a cubierto	*sheltered*
a chorros	*abundantly*
a diferencia de	*unlike*
a duras penas	*with great difficulty*
a escoger	*all at the same price (your choice)*
a escondidas	*in a secret manner, on the sly*

a excepción de	*with the exception of*
a fin de cuentas	*at the end*
a fines de	*at the end of*
a fondo	*thoroughly*
a fuego lento	*on a slow fire*
a fuerza de	*by dint of*
a la antigua	*out of fashion*
a la carrera	*hastily*
a la derecha	*to the right*
a la francesa	*French style*
a la hora de la comida	*at meal time*
a la izquierda	*to the left*
a la larga	*in the long run*
a la ligera	*lightly, not seriously*
a la moda	*in style*
a la mitad	*halfway*
a la orilla de	*at the edge of*
a la par	*equally, jointly*
a la sombra de	*in the shade of*
a la vez	*at the same time, together*
a la vuelta	*around the corner*
a las mil maravillas	*marvelously*
a lo largo de	*along, alongside of*
a lo lejos	*in the distance*
a lo más	*at most*
a lo mejor	*perhaps, maybe*
a lo sumo	*at most*
a los pocos días	*a few days later*
al aire libre	*in the open air, outdoors*
al alcance de	*within reach of*
al año	*after a year*
al azar	*at random*
al cabo de	*at the end of*
al cabo de un rato	*after a while*
al contado	*for cash*
al contrario	*on the contrary*
al corriente	*informed*
al descubierto	*openly*
al día	*up to date*
al día siguiente	*on the following day*
al exterior de	*on the outside of*
al extranjero	*abroad*

al fin	*at last*
al fin y al cabo	*after all*
al final de	*at the end of*
al instante	*immediately*
al lado de	*beside, next to*
al menos	*at least*
al menudeo	*retail*
al natural	*without art or affectation*
al otro día	*on the following day*
al parecer	*apparently*
al pie de	*at the foot of*
al principio	*at the beginning*
al por mayor	*wholesale*
al por menor	*retail*
al reverso	*on the reserse side*
al revés	*inside out, the wrong way, backwards*
al sesgo	*on the bias*
al tanto	*informed*
al vuelo	*on the wing*
a manos llenas	*abundantly, plentifully*
a más tardar	*at the very latest*
a mediados de	*around the middle of*
a medias	*halfway*
a medida que	*while, as*
a menos que	*unless*
a menudo	*often*
a mi punto de vista	*in my opinion*
a obscuras	*in the dark*
a pesar de	*in spite of*
a pie	*on foot*
a plomo	*plumb, perpendicularly*
a poco de	*shortly after*
a propósito	*on purpose, by the way*
a propósito de	*in regard to*
a ratos perdidos	*in leisure hours*
a regañadientes	*reluctantly*
a sabiendas	*knowingly*
a sangre fría	*in cold blood*
a solas	*alone*
a tiempo	*in time, on time*
a toda costa	*at all costs, by any means*
a través	*through, across*

¡a tu (su) salud!	*to your health! , cheers!*
a veces	*sometimes, at times*
a ver	*let's see*
a viva fuerza	*with great resolution*
a voluntad	*at will*

11.4 Los modismos empezando por **de** (Idioms beginning with **de**)

de acuerdo	*O.K., agreed*
de ahora en adelante	*from now on*
de antemano	*beforehand, in advance*
de aquí en adelante	*from now on*
de arriba abajo	*from top to bottom*
de balde	*gratis, free*
de buena fe	*in good faith, sincerely*
de buena gana	*gladly, willingly*
de buenas a primeras	*suddenly*
de cabo a cabo	*from beginning to end*
de carrera	*hastily, rashly*
de concierto	*in agreement*
de corazón	*heartily, sincerely*
de costumbre	*usually*
de cuando en cuando	*from time to time, now and then*
de día	*by day*
de día en día	*from day to day*
de frente	*facing, abreast*
de golpe	*all at once, suddenly*
de golpe y porrazo	*unexpectedly*
de hoy en adelante	*from now on*
de hoy en ocho días	*a week from today*
de improviso	*unexpectedly, suddenly*
de lado (poner)	*aside (to put)*
de lejos	*from a distance, from far*
de lo lindo	*wonderfully, greatly*
de mala gana	*unwillingly*
de mala fe	*deceitfully*
de mala manera	*reluctantly*
de mal en peor	*from bad to worse*
de manera que	*so that*
de memoria	*by heart, from memory*
de modo que	*so that*

de nada	*for no reason, you are welcome*
de ninguna manera	*by no means, absolutely not*
de ningún modo	*by no means, absolutely not*
de noche	*by night*
de nuevo	*again*
de ordinario	*ordinarily, usually*
de otra parte	*on the other hand*
de parte a parte	*through and through*
de parte de	*on one's part*
de pie (estar)	*standing (to be)*
de pies a cabeza	*from head to toe*
de plano	*openly, clearly*
de prisa	*rapidly*
de pronto	*suddenly*
de puntillas	*on tiptoe, softly*
de remate	*irremediably, without hope*
de repente	*suddenly*
de repuesto	*spare, extra*
de segunda mano	*secondhand*
de seguro	*sure, surely, certainly*
de sol a sol	*from sunrise to sunset*
de tal forma que	*in such a way that*
de tal manera que	*in such a way that*
de tal palo tal astilla	*a chip of the old block*
de todas partes	*from all sides*
de todo corazón	*wholeheartedly*
de todos modos	*at any rate, anyway*
de última moda	*in the latest style*
de una forma o de la otra	*in one way or another*
de vacaciones	*on vacation*
de veras	*really, indeed*
de verdad	*truly, in fact*
de vez en cuando	*from time to time, once in a while*
de vuelta (estar)	*back (to be)*

11.5 Los modismos empezando por **en** (Idioms beginning with **en**)

en avión	*by plane*
en balde	*in vain*
en barco	*by boat*
en blanco	*blank*

en breve	shortly, in a little while
en cambio	on the other hand
en camino	under way, on the way
en casa	at home
en coche	by car
en contorno	round about
en cuclillas	in a squatting position
en efecto	in fact, truthfully, as a matter of fact
en el acto	at once, immediately
en el fondo	basically
en el peor de los casos	assuming the worst
en el quinto infierno	miles from anywhere
en el suelo	on the ground
en el teléfono	on the telephone
en fin	finally, at last, in short
en guerra	at war
en huelga	on strike
en la actualidad	at the present time
en marcha (poner)	to start (an engine)
en otoño	in the fall
en particular	particularly
en paz	in peace
en pleno día	in broad daylight
en pleno invierno	in the middle of the winter
en pleno sol	in the hot sun
en pocas palabras	in a few words, in short
en primer lugar	first, in the first place
en punto	exactly, sharp
en realidad	really, actually
en rebeldía	by default
en resumen	in short, briefly
en resumidas cuentas	in short, briefly
en seguida	at once, immediately
en todas partes	everywhere
en torno a	around, about
en tren	by train
en un abrir y cerrar de ojos	in a flash
en venta	for sale
en verano	in the summer
en vez de	instead of
en vigor	in force
en voz alta	aloud

11.6 Los modismos empezando por **por** (Idioms beginning with **por**)

por adelantado	*in advance*
por alto (pasar)	*to overlook, to omit*
por allí	*that way*
por amistad	*out of friendship*
por aquí	*this way*
por casualidad	*by accident, by chance*
por cierto	*indeed*
por consiguiente	*consequently, therefore*
por desgracia	*unfortunately*
por ejemplo	*for instance*
por encima	*over, slightly*
por escrito	*in writing*
por favor	*please*
por fin	*finally*
por las buenas o por las malas	*whether we like it or not*
por lo común	*usually*
por lo general	*generally*
por lo menos	*at least*
por lo pronto	*for the time being*
por lo tanto	*consequently, therefore*
por lo visto	*apparently*
por más que	*no matter how much*
por poco	*nearly, almost*
por si acaso	*if by chance, just in case*
por supuesto	*of course*
por término medio	*on the average*
por todas partes	*everywhere*

11.7 Los modismos empezando por **con** (Idioms beginning with **con**)

con buena salud	*in good health*
con cariño	*fondly, affectionately, kindly*
con el objeto de	*aiming to*
con empeño	*in earnest*
con énfasis	*emphatically*
con esmero	*carefully, with great care*
con cuidado	*carefully*
con descuido	*carelessly, negligently*
con gusto	*gladly, with taste*

con mucho gusto	*with great pleasure, gladly*
con permiso	*excuse me*
con que	*so, thus, then*
con seguridad	*surely, positively*
con tal que	*provided that*
con toda franqueza	*quite frankly*
con todo	*nevertheless*
con todo y eso	*in spite of all*

11.8 Los modismos empezando con otras preposiciones (Idioms beginning with other prepositions)

para atrás	*behind, backwards, in reverse*
para que	*so that*
¿para qué?	*what for?*
sin duda	*no doubt*
sin embargo	*however, nevertheless*
sin más ni más	*without warning, without notice*
sin par	*unequaled*
sin ton ni son	*without rhyme or reason*
sobre aviso (estar)	*cautious, wary*
sobre seguro	*without risk, for certain*
sobre todo	*above all, principally, especially*
sobremanera	*excessively, beyond measure*

12 Las conjunciones y los términos de transición

12.1 Las conjunciones (Conjunctions)

A conjunction is a word which connects words, phrases, or clauses.

A. Subordinating conjunctions

The most common subordinating conjunctions are **que** (*that*), **como** (*as*), and **si** (*if*). Conjunctions are invariable in Spanish. **Que** may not be omitted as its English equivalent may.

Espero **que** vengan.
I hope they will come.

Roberto dice **que** su hermano está enfermo y **que** está en casa.
Robert says (that) his brother is sick and is home.

Tengo **que** trabajar como todo el mundo.
I have to work like everybody else.

Como no estaba yo, ella se aprovechó.
As I wasn't here (there), she took advantage of it.

Ella vendrá **si** se lo pide usted.
She will come if you ask her.

Si uno dice que sí, el otro dice que no.
If one says yes, the other one says no.

(See *Las cláusulas condicionales 40* for the sequence of tenses with *if*-clauses.)

B. Conjunctions expressing time

1. **a medida que**   *while, as*

    A medida que yo avanzaba, él retrocedía.

2. **cada vez que**   *each time that*

[50]

Cada vez que me habla, me pide dinero.

3. **cuando**   *when*

Iré a Madrid **cuando** tenga el dinero.

4. **desde que**   *since*

Llueve **desde que** estoy aquí.

5. **después que**   *after*

Lo hicimos **después que** saliste.

6. **en cuanto**   *as soon as*

Te escribiré **en cuanto** llegue a casa.

7. **mientras**   *while*

Lee esta carta **mientras** está sentado.

8. **mientras que**   *while, but*

Él trabaja, **mientras que** ella no hace nada.

9. **tan pronto como**   *as soon as*

Comerá **tan pronto como** regrese.

C. Principal simple conjunctions

además	*besides*
así	*so, thus*
aunque	*although*
empero	*however*
luego	*then, therefore*
mas	*but, yet, however*
menos	*minus, but*
ni	*neither*
ni . . . ni	*neither . . . nor*
o (u)	*or*
o . . . o	*either . . . or*
ora . . . ora	*now . . . now*
pero	*but, yet*
porque	*because*
pues	*because, therefore, inasmuch*
sea . . . sea	*either . . . or*
sino	*but, yet*

siquiera	*although, though*
y (e)	*and*
ya . . . ya	*now . . . now*

1. **Y** becomes **e** before a noun beginning with **i** or **hi**, except for the diphthong **hie**.

    Hernandez **e** hijos   Fernando **e** Isabel

    But: nieve **y** hielo

2. **O** becomes **u** before a noun beginning with **o** or **ho**.

    Juan tiene siete **u** ocho hijos.   Anacreonte **u** Homero

3. The word *but* is usually expressed by **pero**. **Sino** is used when the first part of a sentence is negative and the second part contradicts it.

    No es rico, **sino** pobre.   No quiere estudiar, **sino** jugar.
    No fuiste tú, **sino** Juan.   No es él, **sino** ella.

    Sino que introduces a clause with a different verb.

    No quiero que me lo **regales**, **sino que** me lo **prestes**.

    Mas must not be confused with **más** (*more*).

    Corre, **mas** no te caigas.   *Run but don't fall.*
    Iré, **mas** no me quedaré.   *I'll go, however I won't stay.*

4. **Porque** is always followed by a verbal expression. To express the English *because* before a noun, use **a causa de, por culpa de, por causa de**, or **por motivo de**.

    No vino **porque** no quiso.
    No vino **a causa de** un disgusto que tuvimos.
    Él no vino **por motivo de** enfermedad.

5. When the conjunction **ni** connects two or more subjects, the verb takes the plural form, unlike its English equivalent.

    Ni Alicia **ni** Roberto hablan francés.
    Neither Alicia nor Roberto speaks French.

D. Conjunctive phrases

Many conjunctions are formed by adding **que** to a preposition, past participle, noun, or adverb.

a condición (de) que	*providing that*
a fin de que	*in order that, so that*
a medida que	*while, as*
a menos que	*unless*
a pesar de todo	*in spite of all, anyhow*
ahora que	*now that*
al contrario	*on the contrary*
antes (de) que	*before, sooner than*
aun así	*yet, even so*
aun cuando	*if, even when*
como si	*as if*
comoquiera que	*no matter how*
con tal (de) que	*provided that*
con todo	*however, yet*
cualquiera que	*whichever*
de cualquier modo	*anyhow*
de manera que	*so that, in a way that*
de modo que	*so that, in a way that*
de suerte que	*so that, in a way*
de tal manera que	*in such a way that*
de todas formas	*anyhow*
desde que	*since*
después (de) que	*after*
dondequiera que	*wherever*
en caso (de) que	*in case*
en vista de que	*whereas, seeing that*
fuera de que	*aside from, besides*
hasta que	*until*
lo mismo que	*just as, like*
más bien	*rather*
mientras que	*while, but*
ni siquiera	*not even*
no obstante	*nevertheless, however*
para que	*in order that, so that*
por consiguiente	*consequently*
por lo contrario	*on the contrary*
por lo tanto	*therefore*
por más que	*however much*
por mucho que	*however much*
por miedo (de) que	*for fear that*
por temor (de) que	*for fear that*
pues que	*since, because, inasmuch as*

puesto que	*since, inasmuch as*
salvo que	*excepting that*
según que	*according to whether*
sin embargo	*however, nevertheless*
sin que	*without*
sino que	*but that, only that*
supuesto que	*since, granting, supposing that*
visto que	*whereas, seeing that*
ya que	*since, inasmuch as*

1. Some conjunctive phrases introduce the subjunctive. (see *El subjuntivo 47.3C-D.*)

a fin de que	*in order that, so that*
antes (de) que	*before, sooner than*
con tal (de) que	*in case that*
de manera que	*so that, in a way that*
de modo que	*so that, in a way that*
en caso (de) que	*in case (that)*
para que	*in order that, so that*
sin que	*without*

2. **Tanto . . . como** expresses the conjunction *both.*

    Tanto el padre **como** la madre son estrictos.

3. **Por** + adjective or adverb + **que** expresses *however* + adjective or adverb.

    No me alcanza el dinero **por mucho que** gane.
    Por insignificante que sea la donación, siempre ayuda.

12.2 Los términos de transición (Transition words)

al fin	*finally, at last*
después	*afterwards*
en fin	*in short*
entonces	*then*
finalmente	*finally*
luego	*next, then*
por fin	*finally, at last*
por último	*finally*
primero	*first*
total	*in short*

13 La inversión

A. In interrogative sentences, the subject is generally placed immediately after the verb.

¿Cómo se **llama usted?**   ¿**Habla usted** español?
¿A qué hora **salió María?**   ¿Quiénes **son ellos?**

B. After a direct quotation, the subject usually follows the explanatory verb.

—Estoy lista, **dijo mi hermana.**
—¿Cuántos años tiene usted? , **preguntó Juan.**
—Me sorprendería mucho, me **contestó el profesor.**

The most common explanatory verbs are:

aconsejar	to advise
afirmar	to affirm, to assert
agregar	to add
contestar	to answer
creer	to believe
decir	to say
escribir	to write
exclamar	to exclaim
llamar	to call
ordenar	to order, to command
pedir	to ask for
pensar	to think
preguntar	to ask
preguntarse	to wonder
recomendar	to recommend, to advise
repetir	to repeat
replicar	to retort, to answer, to reply
responder	to answer, to reply

C. Inversion occurs in sentences beginning with certain adverbs or adverbial phrases.

[55]

apenas	*hardly*
así	*thus*
acaso	*maybe*
quizá, quizás	*maybe*
tal vez	*maybe*
por eso	*therefore*
por lo tanto	*therefore*
por lo menos	*at least*
pronto	*soon*
siempre	*always*

Apenas había terminado el presidente . . .
Quizás haya venido Juan.
Tal vez venga ella mañana.
Siempre te llamaron tus padres.

14 El género y el número de los nombres

In Spanish, a noun is either masculine or feminine, and singular or plural.

14.1 Los nombres masculinos (Masculine nouns)

A. Nouns ending in **-o.**

el libro	el año	el banco	el museo
el centro	el amigo	el camino	el gato

Exceptions: **la mano, la foto** (shortened form of **la fotografía**)

B. Most nouns referring to a masculine person.

el padre	el rey	el hombre	el conde
el cura	el médico	el artista	el pintor
el dentista	el policía	el emperador	el pianista

C. Days of the week and months of the year.

el lunes	el mes de junio
el martes	el mes de diciembre

D. Rivers, seas, oceans, and the cardinal points.

el Amazonas   **el Mediterráneo**   **el Atlántico**   **el Norte**

E. Names of languages and musical notes.

el español   **el francés**   **el fa, el sol, el la, el re**

F. Infinitives used as nouns.

el vivir	*life*
Él es amigo **del buen vivir.**	*He is fond of the good life.*

[57]

el comer	*food, eating*
el saber	*knowledge*
el fumar	*smoking*

G. Certain nouns of Greek origin ending in **-ma**.

el clima	el sistema	el dilema	el drama
el programa	el fantasma	el problema	el tema
el síntoma	el idioma	el poema	el telegrama

H. Nouns ending in **-or** and **-ón** (except those ending in **-ión**).

el motor	el clamor	el amor	el furor
el patrón	el pistón	el montón	el rincón

Exceptions: **la flor, la labor, sor**

14.2 Los nombres femeninos (Feminine nouns)

A. Nouns ending in **-a**.

la ropa	la cama	la silla	la mesa
la playa	la cocina	la escuela	la casa

Exceptions: Certain nouns of Greek origin ending in **-ma** (see *Los nombres masculinos 14.1*); many nouns ending in **-ista** when they refer to a masculine person; and a few other commonly used words such as:

el mapa   el déspota   el planeta   el poeta   el día

B. Nouns that refer to a feminine person.

la madre	la mujer	la escritora	la emperatriz
la estudiante	la artista	la cantante	la periodista

C. All nouns ending in **-sión, -ción, -dad, -tad, -tud**, and **-umbre**.

la pasión	la nación	la ciudad	la libertad
la actitud	la costumbre	la juventud	la cumbre

D. Nouns ending in **-dez** and most of those ending in **-ie** (without accent).

la insipidez	la rapidez	la candidez	la rigidez
la languidez	la flaccidez	la especie	la serie

But:

el pie	*the foot*
el puntapié	*the kick*
el hincapié (hacer)	*to stand firm*

E. Letters of the alphabet.

la a, la che, la jota

14.3 Las formas masculina y femenina de ciertos nombres (Masculine and feminine forms of certain nouns)

Some nouns referring to persons or animals have a masculine and a feminine form.

A. Some nouns in -o change -o to -a to form the feminine.

el muchacho	la muchacha	el niño	la niña
el perro	la perra	el gato	la gata
el hijo	la hija	el tío	la tía

B. Some nouns ending in -**or** or -**ón** add -a to form the feminine.

el profesor   la profesora   el patrón   la patrona

C. In some cases, one form is used for both genders. The article does not vary, and the words **de sexo masculino** or **de sexo femenino**, or **macho** or **hembra** may be added.

una víctima de sexo masculino	una persona de sexo femenino
un canario macho	un canario hembra
una cebra macho	una cebra hembra

But:

Él es un ángel.	**Ella** es un ángel.

D. The masculine and the feminine forms of some nouns are alike and only the article varies.

acróbata	demócrata	aristócrata	hipócrita
amante	cómplice	cliente	intérprete
suicida	homicida	camarada	infanticida
reo	testigo	hereje	indígena
mártir	comensal	estudiante	presidente

All nouns ending in -ista:

artista   turista   socialista   violonista

E.   Some feminine forms are different from the masculine.

el hombre	la mujer
el padre	la madre
el yerno	la nuera
el macho	la hembra
el poeta	la poetisa
el rey	la reina
el emperador	la emperatriz
el actor	la actriz
el sacerdote	la sacerdotisa
el abad	la abadesa
el conde	la condesa
el duque	la duquesa
el príncipe	la princesa
fray	sor
el caballo	la yegua
el gallo	la gallina
el toro	la vaca
el carnero	la oveja

F.   Some nouns have different meanings according to their gender.

el capital	*the capital (money)*	la capital	*the capital (city)*
el guía	*the guide*	la guía	*the guidebook*
el corte	*the cut*	la corte	*the court*
el coma	*the coma (illness)*	la coma	*the coma (punctuation)*
el coral	*the coral*	la coral	*the chorale*
el frente	*the front*	la frente	*the forehead*

14.4 Los nombres compuestos (Compound nouns)

Compound nouns composed of a verb and a noun are usually masculine.

el abrelatas	*the can opener*
el cortaplumas	*the penknife*
el guardarropa	*the wardrobe, checkroom*
el portalámparas	*the electrical socket*

But:

la portabandera   *the flagpole socket*
la guardapuerta   *the storm door*

14.5 El plural de los nombres (Plural of nouns)

A. The plural of a noun ending in an unaccented vowel or an accented **e** is formed by adding -s to the singular.

la casa	las casas	el hombre	los hombres
el río	los ríos	el café	los cafés
el gato	los gatos	el corsé	los corsés

B. The plural of a noun ending in a consonant, **-y**, or an accented vowel (except **e**) is formed by adding **-es** to the singular form.

el papel	los papeles	la canción	las canciones
el examen	los exámenes	el mes	los meses
la ley	las leyes	el rey	los reyes
el rubí	los rubíes	el bambú	los bambúes

Exceptions: papá **papás,** mamá **mamás,** sofá **sofás**

C. The plural of a noun ending in **-z** is formed by changing the **-z** to **-c** and adding **-es.**

el lápiz	los lápices	la cruz	las cruces
la luz	las luces	el pez	los peces

D. Nouns of more than one syllable which end in **-s** are invariable.

la dosis	las dosis	la tesis	las tesis
el paraguas	los paraguas	el lunes	los lunes
la crisis	las crisis	el oasis	los oasis

But: el gas **los gases,** la res **las reses**

E. The plural of a compound noun is usually formed by adding **-s** or **-es.**

el ferrocarril	los ferrocarriles	el puntapié	los puntapiés

Exceptions: el gentilhombre   **los gentileshombres**
                 la ricahembra   **las ricashembras**
                 el hijodalgo   **los hijosdalgo**

F.   Some nouns are not used in the plural form.

| el caos | la nada | la fe | la avaricia |
| la inmortalidad | la caridad | el déficit | la plata |

G.   Some nouns are not used in the singular form.

| las gafas | las pinzas | las nupcias | los víveres |
| los anales | los calzoncillos | los modales | las cosquillas |

H.   Some nouns in their masculine plural form refer to persons of both sexes.

los padres (el padre y la madre)
los señores (el señor y la señora)
los hermanos (el hermano y la hermana)
los reyes (el rey y la reina)

15 Las terminaciones aumentativas, diminutivas y despectivas

15.1 Las terminaciones aumentativas (Augmentative endings)

-ón, -ona   -ote, -ota   -azo, -aza   -acho, -acha

These endings usually imply largeness or impressiveness but are often used to convey a comic or a derogatory effect.

grandota	*huge, bulky*
librote	*large book*
narizón	*large-nosed*
orejona	*big-eared*
hombrazo	*husky fellow*
ricacho	*rich person* (derogatory)

The suffix **-azo** is also used to express the idea of a "blow" or a violent action.

un puñetazo	*fist blow*
un portazo	*door slam*

15.2 Las terminaciones diminutivas (Diminutive endings)

-ito, -ita   -cito, -cita,   -ico, -ica,   -cico, -cica
-uelo, -uela   -illo, -illa   -ín, -ina   -cillo, -cilla

papelito	*slip of paper*
mesita	*small table*
amorcito	*beloved*
mujercita	*little woman*
chicuelo	*youngster*
letrica	*small letter*
pobrecico	*poor devil*
mozuela	*young girl*
casilla	*hut, box, square, compartment*

dolorcillo	*small pain*
peluquín	*toupee, small wig*

15.3 Las terminaciones despectivas (Depreciative endings)

-ucho, -ucha   -aco, -aca   -uco, -uca   -uzo, -uza

hoteluco	*third-class hotel*
casucha	*hovel, decrepit cottage*
pajarraco	*ugly bird*
frailuco	*unimportant monk or friar*
gentuza	*rabble, mob*

16 Los cognados

16.1 Los cognados exactos (Exact cognates)

A number of Spanish and English words have identical or very similar spellings.

A. Adjectives ending in

-al:	capital	normal	principal
-ible:	visible	flexible	posible
-able:	notable	aceptable	adorable
-rior:	anterior	superior	inferior

B. Nouns ending in

-al:	hospital	capital	pedestal
-tor:	motor	doctor	conductor

16.2 Los cognados fácilmente reconocidos (Easily recognizable cognates)

Other cognates have dissimilar endings but are easily recognizable.

A. Nouns

    1.   -ia, -ía   ⟶   *-y*

colonia	*colony*
geología	*geology*
historia	*history*
teoría	*theory*

    2.   -dad, -tad   ⟶   *-ty*

legalidad	*legality*
facultad	*faculty*

[65]

sinceridad   *sincerity*
libertad   *liberty*

3.   -ción ⟶ *-tion*

nación   *nation*
emoción   *emotion*
admiración   *admiration*
situación   *situation*

4.   -aje ⟶ *-age*

pasaje   *passage*
mensaje   *message*
pillaje   *pillage*
coraje   *courage*

5.   -itud ⟶ *-itude*

aptitud   *aptitude*
altitud   *altitude*
solicitud   *solicitude*
actitud   *attitude*

6.   -ismo ⟶ *-ism*

socialismo   *socialism*
realismo   *realism*
naturalismo   *naturalism*
turismo   *turism*

7.   -ista ⟶ *-ist*

fatalista   *fatalist*
artista   *artist*
dentista   *dentist*
pianista   *pianist*

B.   Adverbs

-mente   *-ly*

generalmente   *generally*
legalmente   *legally*
personalmente   *personally*
finalmente   *finally*

C. Adjectives

    1.   -oso, -osa   *-ous*

        curioso   *curious*
        famosa   *famous*
        furioso   *furious*
        numeroso   *numerous*

    2.   -ivo, -iva   *-ive*

        decisivo   *decisive*
        subjetivo   *subjective*
        narrativo   *narrative*
        instintiva   *instinctive*

    3.   -ico, -ica   *-ic, -ical*

        fantástico   *fantastic*
        político   *political*
        dinámico   *dynamic*
        eléctrica   *electric*

D. Verbs

    -izar   *-ize, -yze*

    analizar   *analyze*
    realizar   *realize*
    organizar   *organize*
    simbolizar   *symbolize*

16.3 Los cognados falaces (Deceptive cognates)

actual	*at the present, current*
actualmente	*nowadays*
apreciar	*to esteem, to appreciate*
asistir	*to attend, to be present; to help*
carácter	*temper*
come	*eat, eats*
dice	*says*
el local	*site, premises*
el mate	*checkmate*
el pan	*bread*
el papel	*paper; role*
el personaje	*character*

el pie	*foot*
el resorte	*spring; elasticity*
el solar	*lot, plot of ground*
el taller	*workshop*
el valor	*value; valor*
fastidioso	*annoying, boring*
importar	*to matter, to amount to; to import*
intentar	*to attempt, to try; to intend*
la afección	*affection, disease*
la conferencia	*lecture; conference; phone call*
la desgracia	*misfortune*
la diversión	*amusement*
la dote	*dowry; natural gift*
la joya	*jewel*
la lectura	*reading*
la librería	*bookstore*
la locación	*lease, renting, booking*
la oración	*sentence; prayer*
la renta	*revenue, pension; rent*
la visión	*vision; view*
largo	*long*
las inversiones	*investments; inversions*
los males	*ills, evils*
primer	*first*
quitar	*to remove*
realizar	*to fulfill, to realize (to carry out); to convert into money*
restar	*to deduct, to subtract*
revolver	*to stir up, to mix up*
sale	*goes out*
sensible	*sensitive, perceptible*
simpático	*congenial, nice, likeable*
sin	*without*
ten	*take it*

17 La acentuación ortográfica y el silabeo

17.1 La acentuación (Word stress and accents)

In Spanish there is a definite set of rules indicating word stress. When there is an exception to the rules, a written accent mark is used to show the stress.

A. Words ending in a vowel, **n**, or **s** are stressed on the next to the last syllable.

ma-dre	za-**pa**-to	**ca**-sa	**li**-bro	**si**-lla
ha-blan	**o**-jos	**ca**-sas	co-**mie**-ron	**lu**-nes

B. Words ending in a consonant other than **n** or **s** are stressed on the last syllable.

ca-li-**dad**	ha-**blar**	ca-pi-**tal**	e-le-men-**tal**	a-**mor**
so-li-ci-**tud**	al-re-de-**dor**	sin-ce-ri-**dad**	ve-**jez**	re-**loj**

C. Words not conforming to the above rules have a written accent over the vowel which is stressed.

ar-**tí**-cu-lo	**mú**-si-ca	con-tes-**tó**	at-**mós**-fe-ra	**pá**-ja-ro
ár-bol	lec-**ción**	cor-**tés**	jar-**dín**	**hués**-ped

D. Monosyllabic words generally do not need an accent mark.

ver   ser   pie   ley   fue   fui   hay   hoy   vio

E. If a syllable bearing a written accent contains a diphthong—the combination of a strong vowel (**a, o, e**) and a weak vowel (**i, u**), or two weak vowels which form one syllable—the strong vowel prevails over the weak one and takes the accent mark.

des-**pués**   pun-ta-**pié**   re-**cién**   tam-**bién**   pe-**rió**-di-co

An accented weak vowel and an adjacent strong vowel form two separate syllables.

po-es-í-a   te-ní-a   le-í-do   sa-bí-a-mos   po-drí-an   o-ís-te
dí-a   tí-o   rí-o   mí-o   dí-as   mí-as   tí-a   dú-o

Two strong vowels do not constitute a diphthong but are considered as two separate syllables.

le-er   cre-er   ma-re-o   pla-ne-ar   hé-ro-e

F.   A diacritical accent is used to distinguish between two words which are written the same but have different meanings.

1.   Monosyllabic words

dé	give (command)	de	of, from
tú	you	tu	your
él	he, him	el	the
mí	me	mi	my
sí	yes	si	if
sé	I know; be (command)	se	oneself
más	more	mas	but

2.   Demonstrative pronouns   Demonstrative adjectives

éste	this one	este	this
ése	that one	ese	that
aquél	that one (over there)	aquel	that (over there)

3.   Interrogatives   Relatives

¿cuándo?	when?	cuando	when
¿cuánto?	how much?	cuanto	how much
¿cuál?	which?	cual	which
¿cómo?	how?	como	how
¿dónde?	where?	donde	where
¿qué?	what?	que	what, that
¿quién?	who?, whom?	quien	who, whom

17.2 El silabeo (Syllabication)

A.   A single consonant (including ch, ll, rr) between two vowels forms a syllable with the following vowel.

te-lé-fo-no   ca-lle   mu-cha-cha   ca-rro

B.   Generally two consonants within a word are divided.

ac-ti-tud   **ac-ción**   **ig-no-ran-cia**   **cal-ma**

C.   The following combinations whose second consonant is l or r are not
      separated.

br, cr, dr, fr, gr, pr, tr, bl, cl, fl, gl, pl, tl
des-cu-**br**ir   cua-**dr**o   des-**cr**i-bir   re-**fr**es-car
a-**pr**e-tar   ca-**bl**e   a-**pl**a-nar   a-**tl**e-ta

D.   The vowels in a diphthong—the combination of a strong vowel (**a, o, e**)
      and a weak vowel (**i, u**) or two weak vowels—are not separated.

he-**roi**-co   **bai**-le   **pier**-den   en-su-**ciar**

E.   An accented weak vowel and an adjacent strong vowel form two sepa-
      rate syllables.

te-ní-a   le-í-do   sa-bí-a-mos   o-ís-te

F.   A triphthong—a strong vowel preceded and followed by weak vowel—is
      considered one syllable.

a-pre-**ciáis**   U-ru-**guay**   a-ve-ri-**guáis**   b**uey**

G.   Two adjacent strong vowels do not constitute a diphthong. They are
      separated into two syllables.

le-er   **a**-or-ta   em-ple-**ado**   cam-pe-**ón**

H.   There are several rules for the separation of syllables at the end of a
      written or printed line.

      1.   Two vowels are not separated, although they may form two dis-
            tinct syllables.

            pro-veer   and not   **prove-er**
            leer   and not   **le-er**

      2.   Vowels are not written without a consonant.

            te-nía   and not   **tení-a**
            apre-tar   and not   **a-pretar**
            atle-ta   and not   **a-tleta**
            euro-peo   and not   **eu-ropeo**

3.   If a consonant precedes an **h**, the letters are separated.

des-hacer   in-humano   al-haja

4.   In compound words, it is preferable to separate the two components.

corta-plumas   punta-pié   ferro-carril   sobre-todo

5.   Note that s + a consonant does not begin a word or a syllable in Spanish.

18 Los pronombres

In Spanish, as in English, there are various kinds of pronouns: personal, possessive, demonstrative, relative, indefinite, negative, interrogative, and exclamatory.

A pronoun is a word used in the place of or as a substitute for a noun. In Spanish, it reflects the person, gender, and number of its antecedent or of the word it replaces.

18.1 Los pronombres personales (Personal pronouns)

A. Subject pronouns

yo	*I*	nosotros (-as)	*we*
tú	*you*	vosotros (-as)	*you*
él	*he, it*	ellos	*they*
ella	*she, it*	ellas	*they*
usted (Vd., Ud.)	*you*	ustedes (Vds., Uds.)	*you*

1. **Tú** and **vosotros**, both meaning *you*, are the familiar forms used to address children, relatives, close friends, and pets. In Latin America, the pronoun **ustedes** is generally used instead of **vosotros**. **Usted** and **ustedes** are the more conventional or formal forms meaning *you*. They are used with a verb in the third person.

2. Omission of the subject pronoun

    Since the Spanish verb endings indicate the person or persons performing the action, the subject pronoun is omitted unless needed for emphasis or clarity. **Usted** and **ustedes** are usually expressed, although excessive repetition is avoided.

    Puedo hacerlo.
    Yo puedo hacerlo; **tú** no puedes.
    Iba a la escuela todos los días.
    Yo iba a la escuela todos los días; mi hermana no.
    Siempre que **él** decía que sí, **ella** decía que no.

[73]

3.   The subject pronoun is used

a.   In comparisons.

Carlos es más fuerte que **tú**.

b.   In answers without a verb.

¿Quién es?   —**Yo**.   ¿Quién ganó?   —**Él**.

c.   After the verb **ser**.

¿Fuiste **tú** quién me llamó?   —Sí, fui **yo**.

d.   When separated from the verb.

Ellas solas fueron culpables.

e.   For emphasis with the adjective **mismo**.

Yo mismo se lo mandé.
Háganlo **ustedes mismos**.

f.   In compound subjects.

Fuimos **él y yo**.
Fernando y yo nos quedamos con las ganas.

B.   Direct object pronouns

Él **me** conoce.	Él **nos** conoce.
He knows me.	*He knows us.*
Él **te** conoce.	Él **os** conoce.
He knows you.	*He knows you.*
Él **(le), lo, la** conoce.	Él **los, las** conoce.
He knows him, her, you, it.	*He knows them, you.*

1.   The direct object pronoun stands for an object that receives the action of the verb without the means of a preposition. It answers the questions "what? " or "whom? "

2.   Note that **le** refers only to a person and, although used frequently in Spain, it is seldom used as a direct object pronoun in Spanish-American countries.

Lo, la, los, and **las** are used for things and persons. The pronoun **lo** sometimes stands for an idea:

¿Sabía usted que **cambiaron el horario?**   —No, no **lo** sabía.
¿**Cuándo saldrá** Manuela de viaje?   —Pregúnteselo a ella.

C.   Indirect object pronouns

Él **me** escribe.	Él **nos** escribe.
He writes to me.	*He writes to us.*
Él **te** escribe.	Él **os** escribe.
He writes to you.	*He writes to you.*
Él **le** escribe.	Él **les** escribe.
He writes to him, to her, to you.	*He writes to them, to you.*

1.   The indirect object pronoun stands for an object that receives the action of the verb by means of the preposition **a**, not to be confused with the "personal a". (See *La preposición personal* **a** *19*.) It answers the questions "to what? " or "to whom? "

2.   The indirect object pronouns **le** and **les** both change to **se** when preceding the direct object pronouns **lo, la, los,** or **las** to avoid cacophony.

   ~~Le~~ lo = **se lo**   Él **se lo** leyó. *He read it to him, to her, to you.*
   ~~Les~~ lo = **se lo** Él **se lo** leyó. *He read it to them, to you.*

3.   The indirect object pronouns **le, les,** or **se** are clarified by the addition of the preposition **a** and the pronouns used after a preposition. (See *Los pronombres 18.1D*.)

   Le expliqué el cuento **a él, a ella, a usted.**
   Les pago **a ellos, a ellas, a ustedes.**
   Se lo regalé **a él, a ella, a ellos, a ellas, a usted, a ustedes.**

4.   The indirect object pronoun is generally used even though the indirect object is otherwise stated.

   Le doy las flores **a María.**

5.   The indirect object pronoun is used with many verbs in Spanish although no preposition is used with the corresponding English verb.

contestar(le) a una persona	*to answer a person*
preguntar(le) (algo) a una persona	*to ask a person (something)*
asustar(le) a una persona	*to scare a person*
sorprender(le) a una persona	*to surprise a person*
enseñar(le) (algo) a una persona	*to teach, to show a person (something)*
mostrar(le) (algo) a una persona	*to show a person (something)*
dar(le) (algo) a una persona	*to give a person (something)*
vender(le) (algo) a una persona	*to sell a person (something)*

enviar(le) (algo) a una persona   *to send a person (something)*
prestar(le) (algo) a una persona   *to lend a person (something)*
escribir(le) a una persona   *to write to a person*
traer(le) (algo) a una persona   *to bring a person (something)*

D.   Prepositional pronouns

para **mí**	*for me*	para **nosotros** (-as)	*for us*
para **ti**	*for you*	para **vosotros** (-as)	*for you*
para **él**	*for him*	para **ellos**	*for them*
para **ella**	*for her*	para **ellas**	*for them*
para **usted**	*for you*	para **ustedes**	*for you*
para **sí**	*for oneself, himself, herself, yourself*	para **sí**	*for themselves, yourselves*

1.   Except for **mí**, **ti**, and **sí**, prepositional pronouns are the same as subject pronouns. The pronoun **mí** bears an accent mark to distinguish it from the possessive adjective **mi**.

2.   When used with the preposition **con**, the forms **mí**, **ti**, and the reflexive **sí** (used as object of a preposition) become **conmigo**, **contigo**, and **consigo** respectively. All other forms remain unaltered.

Fui **con ella** al cine.   Ella fue **conmigo** al cine.

3.   The prepositional phrases **a mí**, **a ti**, **a él**, **a usted**, and so on are used in addition to the direct or indirect object pronouns for purposes of clarification or emphasis.

No **se** lo dio **a usted**; **me** lo dio **a mí**.
La llamaré **a ella**, no **a usted**.

4.   After the prepositions **entre** and **según**, subject pronouns are used.

Según ellos, no vendrán a la fiesta.
Entre tú y yo, sin ella no puedo vivir.

E.   Reflexive pronouns

me lavo	**nos** lavamos
I wash myself	*we wash ourselves*
te lavas	**os** laváis
you wash yourself	*you wash yourselves*

se lava   se lavan
he (she) washes himself (herself)   *they wash themselves*
you wash yourself   *you wash yourselves*

Reflexive pronouns are used with reflexive verbs and may be direct or indirect objects. (See also *Los verbos reflexivos 44*.) The reflexive pronoun **se** may act as direct or indirect object pronoun of the third person for both genders, plural and singular.

F.   Table of personal pronouns

SUBJECT	PREPOSITIONAL	REFLEXIVE	INDIRECT OBJECT	DIRECT OBJECT
yo	mí	me	me	me
tú	ti	te	te	te
él	él, sí	se	le (se)	le, lo
ella	ella, sí	se	le (se)	la
usted	usted, sí	se	le (se)	le, lo, la
nosotros (-as)	nosotros (-as)	nos	nos	nos
vosotros (-as)	vosotros (-as)	os	os	os
ellos	ellos, sí	se	les (se)	los
ellas	ellas, sí	se	les (se)	las
ustedes	ustedes, sí	se	les (se)	los, las

G.   Placement of personal pronouns

1.   An object pronoun normally precedes the conjugated verb.

Me levanto a las ocho.   **Nos** dieron la noticia.
Ella se lo dijo.   Él **me la** dio.

2.   An object pronoun follows and is attached

a.   To affirmative commands.

Déme usted el libro.   **Démelo** usted.
Hágame el favor de cerrar la puerta.   Hágalo usted.

In negative commands, however, the object pronoun precedes the verb and is placed between the negative word and the verb.

Nunca **me** digas eso.   No **lo** haga usted.

b.   To the infinitive when the pronoun is object of the infinitive.

Quiero leer**lo** antes de dár**selo**.
Lo pensó mucho antes de comprar**lo**.

An object pronoun may also precede the conjugated forms of verbs followed by an infinitive.

Lo quiero leer antes de dárselo.	*or*	Quiero leer**lo** antes de dárselo.
Se lo voy a dar.	*or*	Voy a dár**selo**.
Le tengo que pagar.	*or*	Tengo que pagar**le**.
Le puedo escribir mañana.	*or*	Puedo escribir**le** mañana.

c.   To the present participle (**gerundio**).

Escuchánd**ola**, se durmió.
Conociénd**olos** como los conozco, sé que son incapaces de mentir.

An object pronoun may be attached to the present participle or used before the verb **estar** in the progressive forms.

Lo está estudiando.	*or*	Está estudiándo**lo**.
Las estábamos mirando.	*or*	Estábamos mirándo**las**.

18.2 Los pronombres posesivos (Possessive pronouns)

mi libro *my book*	**el mío** *mine*	mi llave *my key*	**la mía** *mine*
tu libro *your book*	**el tuyo** *yours*	tu llave *your key*	**la tuya** *yours*
su libro *his, her, your book*	**el suyo** *his, hers, yours*	su llave *his, her, your key*	**la suya** *his, hers, yours*
mis libros *my books*	**los míos** *mine*	mis llaves *my keys*	**las mías** *mine*
tus libros *your books*	**los tuyos** *yours*	tus llaves *your keys*	**las tuyas** *yours*
sus libros *his, her, your books*	**los suyos** *his, hers, yours*	sus llaves *his, her, your keys*	**las suyas** *his, hers, yours*

nuestro libro	**el nuestro**	nuestra llave	**las nuestras**
our book	*ours*	*our key*	*ours*
vuestro libro	**el vuestro**	vuestra llave	**la vuestra**
your book	*yours*	*your key*	*yours*
su libro	**el suyo**	su llave	**la suya**
their, your book	*theirs, yours*	*their key*	*theirs, yours*
nuestros libros	**los nuestros**	nuestras llaves	**las nuestras**
our books	*ours*	*our keys*	*ours*
vuestros libros	**los vuestros**	vuestras llaves	**las vuestras**
your books	*yours*	*your keys*	*yours*
sus libros	**los suyos**	sus llaves	**las suyas**
their, your books	*theirs, yours*	*their, your keys*	*theirs, yours*

A.   A possessive pronoun replaces a noun modified by a possessive adjective.

B.   After the verb **ser**, the definite article is generally not used.

Este dinero **es mío**.   Ese coche no **es tuyo**.

But:

No es **el tuyo** el que perdí, sino **el mío**.

C.   A prepositional phrase is used instead of **el suyo, la suya, los suyos, las suyas** when clarification is necessary.

el de él	la de él	los de él	las de él
el de ella	la de ella	los de ella	las de ella
el de usted	la de usted	los de usted	las de usted
el de ellos	la de ellos	los de ellos	las de ellos
el de ellas	la de ellas	los de ellas	las de ellas
el de ustedes	la de ustedes	los de ustedes	las de ustedes

mi libro y **el de él**   *my book and his*
nuestro libro y **el de ella**   *our book and hers*

D.   With the neuter article **lo**, the possessive pronouns acquire an abstract sense.

lo mío   *what is mine*
lo suyo   ·   *what is his, hers, yours*

18.3 Los pronombres demostrativos (Demonstrative pronouns)

este·libro	**éste**	esta silla	**ésta**	*this one*
ese libro	**ése**	esa silla	**ésa**	*that one*
aquel libro	**aquél**	aquella silla	**aquélla**	*that one* (far)
estos libros	**éstos**	estas sillas	**éstas**	*these*
esos libros	**ésos**	esas sillas	**ésas**	*those*
aquellos libros	**aquéllos**	aquellas sillas	**aquéllas**	*those* (far)

A.   Demonstrative pronouns are the same as demonstrative adjectives except that they bear a written accent to distinguish them.

B.   Neuter demonstrative pronouns

1.   Because neuter demonstrative pronouns do not have corresponding adjective forms, no written accent is necessary.

esto	*this*
eso	*that*
aquello	*that* (far)

2.   These pronouns are invariable and refer to general ideas already mentioned or to things not well defined.

Esto molesta.	*This bothers me.*
Eso no me interesa.	*That does not interest me.*
Aquello sucedió ayer.	*That happened yesterday.*
¡Eso es!	*That's it!*

3.   When the neuter demonstrative pronoun is followed by the preposition **de**, it expresses *the idea of, this business of.*

Eso de ser pobre es una desgracia.
To be poor is a misfortune. (That business of being poor . . .)

Esto de comer a toda hora engorda mucho.
To eat at all hours makes you gain weight. (This business . . .)

C.   The demonstrative pronoun **éste** is used to indicate *the latter*, and **aquél**, *the former*. When both are mentioned, **éste** comes first.

Juan y María son dos personas interesantes; **ésta** es simpática, **aquél** no.

18.4 Los pronombres y los adjetivos.relativos (Relative pronouns and adjectives)

que	*which, that, who, whom*
quien, quienes	*who, whom*
el cual, la cual, los cuales, las cuales	*which, that, who, whom*
el que, la que, los que, las que	*the one who, the ones who*
lo cual, lo que	*that which, which*
cuyo, cuya, cuyos, cuyas	*whose*

A relative pronoun introduces a clause which is in "relation" to a word in the principal clause; this word is called an *antecedent.* Relative pronouns are not omitted in Spanish as their English equivalents may be.

A.   **Que** (*which, that, who, whom*) is the most frequently used of the relative pronouns. It is used for persons and things and functions as subject or direct object of the verb in the dependent clause. Its form is invariable.

La persona **que** llamó no dejó su nombre.
The person who called didn't leave his name.

El coche **que** está frente a mi casa no me pertenece.
The car which is in front of my house does not belong to me.

Los zapatos **que** queremos comprar valen mucho.
The shoes we want to buy are expensive.

Me gustan mucho las historias **que** cuenta ella.
I like very much the stories she is telling.

When **que** is preceded by a preposition, it refers only to things.

La pintura **de que** te hablé fue vendida ayer.
The painting I spoke to you about was sold yesterday.

B.   **Quien(es)** (*who, whom*) refers only to persons and is usually preceded by a preposition. The most common prepositions are **a, con, de, en**, and **para**.

Los hombres **de quienes** hemos hablado son artistas.
The men of whom we spoke are artists.

La mujer **con quien** se casó era viuda.
The woman he married was a widow.

La señora **a quien** se refiere usted está enferma.
The lady you are referring to is sick.

There is no feminine form of this pronoun. **Quien** also appears frequently when a distinction must be made between a person and a thing.

El dueño de la casa, **quien** se cayó hace poco . . .
The owner of the house, who fell a while back . . .

C.   **El cual (la cual, los cuales, las cuales**–*which, that, who, whom*) and **el que (la que, los que, las que**–*the one who, the ones who*) may be used instead of **que** for things and **quien(es)** for persons

1.   To clarify the reference.

El hijo de Juana, **el cual (el que)** estaba enfermo . . .
Juana's son, the one who was sick . . .

Las hermanas de mis amigos, **las cuales (las que)** no he visto . . .
My friends' sisters, whom I haven't seen . . . (ambiguous in English)

2.   After prepositions of two or more syllables and usually after the prepositions **sin** and **por**.

El coche **detrás del**[1] **cual** estaban jugando . . .
The car behind which they were playing . . .

La puerta **por la cual** habían salido . . .
The door through which they left . . .

He perdido los libros **sin los cuales** no puedo estudiar.
I lost the books without which I cannot study.

Los estudiantes **contra los cuales** tienen que jugar son fuertes.
The students against whom they have to play are strong.

Note that **el que (la que, los que, las que)** may not be substituted by **el cual (la cual, los cuales, las cuales)** when the definite article **el (la, los, las)** serves as the only antecedent of the relative pronoun **que**.

La que lleva la falda corta es una amiga de mi primo.
The one wearing the short skirt is a friend of my cousin.

Los que vinieron se divirtieron.
The ones who came had fun.

D.   **lo que** and **lo cual**

If the relative pronoun **que** (subject or object) has no noun or pronoun antecedent, it is used with **lo**, which functions as antecedent.

---

1. **El** contracts with **de** to form **del** and with **a** to form **al**.

Sé **lo que** le molesta.
I know what bothers you.

Dígame **lo que** le interesa.
Tell me what interests you.

Lo que yo quisiera es un nuevo coche.
What I want is a new car.

No oí **lo que** explicó el profesor.
I didn't hear what the professor explained.

Lo que and **lo cual** may be used interchangeably to express the English *which*, when referring to an idea previously mentioned.

No vino a la fiesta, **lo que (lo cual)** me parece extraño.
He (she) didn't come to the party, which seems strange to me.

Trabajé bien, de **lo que (lo cual)** estoy contento.
I worked well, for which I am happy.

Llovió toda la semana, **lo cual (lo que)** no me agradó mucho.
It rained all week, which didn't please me much.

Lo que is used instead of the interrogative form **¿qué?** in reported speech. (See also *El estilo indirecto 45*.)

¿**Qué** le interesa?   *What interests you?*
Me preguntó **lo que** me interesaba. *He asked me what I was interested in.*

E.   The relative adjective **cuyo (cuya, cuyos, cuyas**—*whose*) agrees in gender and number with the noun it modifies.

El hombre, **cuya hija** murió, es amigo mío.
Éste es el artista **cuyos cuadros** compramos el año pasado.
El escritor, **cuyas obras** leyeron ayer, es muy famoso.

F.   The expression **todo lo que** (*all that*) may be substituted by **cuanto**.

Todo lo que tengo es tuyo.   **Cuanto** tengo es tuyo.
Ella da **todo lo que** tiene.   Ella da **cuanto** tiene.

G.   **Donde** often replaces a preposition + a relative pronoun indicating a position.

la mesa **donde (sobre la cual)** dejé mis libros
la casa **donde (en la cual, en la que)** vivimos

18.5 Los pronombres indefinidos y negativos (Indefinite and negative pronouns)

Some indefinite pronouns are also used as indefinite adjectives. (See also *Los adjetivos indefinidos 4.6.*

A.   **uno, una, unos, unas** (*one, some*)

This pronoun indicates that the action is done or received by one or several unspecified persons.

Uno nunca sabe.
Uno no debe ser egoísta si quiere tener amigos.
Siempre hay **unos** que no quieren trabajar.

B.   **alguno, alguna, algunos, algunas** (*someone, some of them*)

Algunos fueron al concierto.
Leí muchas novelas; **algunas** me gustaron.

C.   **ninguno, ninguna** (*no one*) (See also *Los palabras negativas y afirmativas 3.2.*)

Ninguno extendió la explicación.
Ninguna quiso venir a mi casa.

D.   **varios, varias** (*several*)

Tengo **varias** en mi biblioteca.
Necesitamos **varios** para este trabajo.

E.   **otro, otra, otros, otras** (*other, another, others*)

Otra en su lugar se hubiera quedado.
Uno lloró, el **otro** se quejó.
Unos se divierten, **otros** estudian.

F.   **todo, toda, todos, todas** (*everything, all, all of them*)

Lo entiendo **todo**.	*I understand everything.*
La leí **toda** *(la carta).*	*I read it all.*
Todos vinieron.	*They all came.*

G.   **mismo, misma, mismos, mismas** (*the same one, the same ones*).

As a pronoun, **mismo** is preceded by the definite article.

¿Son las mismas personas?   —Sí, son **las mismas.**
No es el libro que te presté.   —Sí, es **el mismo.**

H.   **poco, poca, pocos, pocas** (*a little, a few*)

Había muchos pasajeros en este avión, pero **pocos** se salvaron.
Mucho quieres y **poco** tengo.

I.   **mucho, mucha, muchos, muchas** (*a lot, a lot of them*)

Me gustan **muchas** pero consigo pocas.
Mucho pides y nada das.

J.   **cualquiera, cualesquiera** (*anyone, anybody*)

Daremos ayuda a **cualquiera.**
Démelos, **cualesquiera** que sean.

K.   **quienquiera, quienesquiera** (*anyone, anybody, whoever*)

Quienquiera que venga encontrará puerta abierta.
Quienesquiera que sean, no los permita entrar.

L.   **demasiado, demasiada, demasiados, demasiadas** (*too much, too many*)

He visto **demasiado** en mi vida.
Vinieron **demasiados** a la fiesta.

M.   **bastante, bastantes** (*enough, enough of them*)

No compres más; ya tienes **bastantes.**

N.   **demás** (*the rest, the others*)

This form is preceded by **lo, los,** or **las.**

Por **lo demás,** ¿quién sabe?   *For the rest, who knows?*
Ya escribí a **los demás.**   *I already wrote the others.*

O.   **ambos, ambas** (*both*)

Ambos contestaron a mi carta.

P.   **alguien** (*somebody*)

This pronoun is invariable and purely pronominal.

Alguien me llamó por teléfono.

Q.   **nadie** (*nobody*)

This form is invariable and purely pronominal. (See also *Las palabras negativas y afirmativas 3.2.*)

No conozco a **nadie** en esta ciudad.
Nadie me llamó.

R.   **algo** (*something*)

This form is invariable and purely pronominal.

¿Dijiste **algo**?
¿Tiene **algo** bueno para comer?

S.   **nada** (*nothing*)

This form is invariable and purely pronominal. (See also *Las palabras negativas y afirmativas 3.2.*)

No compré **nada** cuando fui a España.
No me preguntaron **nada** cuando pasé la frontera.

18.6 Los pronombres interrogativos (Interrogative pronouns)

The interrogative pronoun always has a written accent.

A.   **¿qué?** (*what?*) For things only.

¿Qué compraste ayer?
¿De **qué** hablaban?

B.   **¿quién?** , **¿quiénes?** (*who?* , *whom?*) For persons only.

¿Quién llamó esta mañana?
¿A **quién** pidieron ayuda?
¿Quiénes son los culpables?
¿De **quién** habló usted?

¿de quién + ser . . . ? (*whose?*)

¿De quién es este libro?
¿De quién era la carta que recibiste?

C.   ¿cuál? , ¿cuáles? (*which? , which ones?*) For persons and things.

¿**Cuál** es la mía?
¿**Cuál** de los dos toca la guitarra?
¿**Cuáles** son los mejores automóviles?

D.   ¿cuánto? , ¿cuánta? , ¿cuántos? , ¿cuántas? (*how much?*, *how many?*)

¿**Cuántos** fueron a la reunión?
¿**Cuánto** piden por su coche?

E.   The interrogative pronoun retains the written accent in indirect discourse (see *El estilo indirecto 45*), or in a sentence so phrased that it refers to a question either in the mind of the speaker or in that of the person addressed.

Luisa me preguntó **quién** era esa mujer.
Dime **cuál** prefieres.
No quiero decir **quién** es este señor.

18.7 Los pronombres exclamativos o admirativos (Exclamatory pronouns)

Most interrogatives may be used in exclamations. The exclamatory word also has a written accent and is preceded by an inverted exclamation mark.

¡**Qué** pelea!	*What a fight!*
¡**Qué** guapa eres!	*How beautiful you are!*
¡**Cuánto** me alegro!	*How happy I am!*
¡**Quién** lo hubiera dicho!	*Who would have said (thought) it!*
¡**Cuánto** lo siento!	*How sorry I am!*

When an adjective follows the noun, **tan** or **más** is used before the adjective.

¡Qué hombre **tan (más)** simpático!

After the exclamation ¡**Ojalá (que)!** (*I wish!, I hope!*), the subjunctive is used. (See also *El presente de subjuntivo 47.3L*.)

¡**Ojalá** que llueva!	*I hope it rains!*
¡**Ojalá** que vinieran!	*I wish they would come!*

19 La preposición personal *a*

A. The preposition **a** (called the personal **a**) is used before a direct object that refers to a specific person, persons, or a personified object, except after the verb **tener.**

Buscamos **a nuestros amigos.**	*We looked for our friends.*
Encontré **a mi madre** en el parque.	*I found my mother in the park.*
Tememos **a la pobreza.**	*We fear poverty.*

But:

Tengo dos hermanas.

B. The personal **a** is also used when the direct object is one of the indefinites referring to persons: **alguien, nadie, alguno(s), alguna(s), ninguno(s), ninguna(s).**

¿Ha visto usted **a alguien?**
No he llamado **a nadie.**
Conocemos **a algunos** de ellos.

C. The personal **a** is generally not used when the direct object does not refer to a specific person.

Busco una secretaria.

But: Busco **a mi secretaria.**

Las mayúsculas
20 y las minúsculas

Capital letters are less frequently used in Spanish than in English.

A. Capitalize only

  1. The first word in a sentence.
  2. Proper names of persons, animals, countries, cities, rivers, mountains, and other geographical locations.
  3. Abbreviations such as **Vd., Ud., Vds., Uds., Dr., Dra., Sr., Sra., Srta., D., Da.**

B. Do not capitalize

  1. Days of the week.   Hoy es **lunes.**
  2. Months.   Iré a Madrid en **enero.**
  3. Languages.   El **español** no es difícil.
  4. Nationalities.   Es un escritor **francés.**
  5. Religions.   Somos **católicos.**
  6. Members of political parties.   Mi tío es **socialista.**
  7. **Yo**, unless it begins a sentence.

C. Accent marks need not appear on capital letters. The tilde, however, which is an integral part of the letter **ñ**, may not be deleted.

21 El verbo <u>estar</u> (to be)

INDICATIVO (*Indicative*)

	PRESENTE (*Present*)	IMPERFECTO (*Imperfect*)	PRETÉRITO (*Preterit*)	FUTURO (*Future*)
yo	estoy	estaba	estuve	estaré
tú	estás	estabas	estuviste	estarás
él, ella, usted	está	estaba	estuvo	estará
nosotros	estamos	estábamos	estuvimos	estaremos
vosotros	estáis	estabais	estuvisteis	estaréis
ellos, ellas, ustedes	están	estaban	estuvieron	estarán

	PERFECTO (*Present perfect*)	PLUSCUAMPERFECTO (*Pluperfect*)
yo	he estado	había estado
tú	has estado	habías estado
él, ella, usted	ha estado	había estado
nosotros	hemos estado	habíamos estado
vosotros	habéis estado	habíais estado
ellos, ellas, ustedes	han estado	habían estado

	PRETÉRITO ANTERIOR (*Preterit perfect*)	FUTURO PERFECTO (*Future perfect*)
yo	hube estado	habré estado
tú	hubiste estado	habrás estado
él, ella, usted	hubo estado	habrá estado
nosotros	hubimos estado	habremos estado
vosotros	hubisteis estado	habréis estado
ellos, ellas, ustedes	hubieron estado	habrán estado

CONDICIONAL (*Conditional*)

	SIMPLE	PERFECTO (*Conditional perfect*)
yo	estaría	habría estado
tú	estarías	habrías estado
él, ella, usted	estaría	habría estado
nosotros	estaríamos	habríamos estado
vosotros	estaríais	habríais estado
ellos, ellas, ustedes	estarían	habrían estado

IMPERATIVO Y MANDATOS (*Imperative and commands*)

(tú)	está
(usted)	esté
(nosotros)	estemos
(vosotros)	estad
(ustedes)	estén

SUBJUNTIVO (*Subjunctive*)

	PRESENTE (*Present*)	IMPERFECTO (*Imperfect*)	
yo	esté	estuviera	estuviese
tú	estés	estuvieras	estuvieses
él, ella, usted	esté	estuviera	estuviese
nosotros	estemos	estuviéramos	estuviésemos
vosotros	estéis	estuvierais	estuvieseis
ellos, ellas, ustedes	estén	estuvieran	estuviesen

	PERFECTO (*Present perfect*)	PLUSCUAMPERFECTO (*Pluperfect*)
yo	haya estado	hubiere, hubiese estado
tú	hayas estado	hubieras, hubieses estado
él, ella, usted	haya estado	hubiera, hubiese estado
nosotros	hayamos estado	hubiéramos, hubiésemos estado
vosotros	hayáis estado	hubierais, hubieseis estado
ellos, ellas, ustedes	hayan estado	hubieran, hubiesen estado

INFINITIVO (*Infinitive*)

    PRESENTE: **estar**   PRETÉRITO (*Perfect*): **haber estado**

GERUNDIO

    PRESENTE (*Present participle*):   **estando**
    PRETÉRITO (*Perfect participle*):   **habiendo estado**

PARTICIPIO PASIVO (*Past participle*):   **estado**

22 El verbo <u>ser</u> (to be)

INDICATIVO (*Indicative*)

	PRESENTE (*Present*)	IMPERFECTO (*Imperfect*)	PRETÉRITO (*Preterit*)	FUTURO (*Future*)
yo	soy	era	fui	seré
tú	eres	eras	fuiste	serás
él, ella, usted	es	era	fue	será
nosotros	somos	éramos	fuimos	seremos
vosotros	sois	erais	fuisteis	seréis
ellos, ellas, ustedes	son	eran	fueron	serán

	PERFECTO (*Present Perfect*)	PLUSCUAMPERFECTO (*Pluperfect*)
yo	he sido	había sido
tú	has sido	habías sido
él, ella, usted	ha sido	había sido
nosotros	hemos sido	habíamos sido
vosotros	habéis sido	habíais sido
ellos, ellas, ustedes	han sido	habían sido

	PRETÉRITO ANTERIOR (*Preterit perfect*)	FUTURO PERFECTO (*Future perfect*)
yo	hube sido	habré sido
tú	hubiste sido	habrás sido
él, ella, usted	hubo sido	habrá sido
nosotros	hubimos sido	habremos sido
vosotros	hubisteis sido	habréis sido
ellos, ellas, ustedes	hubieron sido	habrán sido

CONDICIONAL (*Conditional*)

	SIMPLE	PERFECTO (*Conditional perfect*)
yo	sería	habría sido
tú	serías	habrías sido
él, ella, usted	sería	habría sido
nosotros	seríamos	habríamos sido
vosotros	seríais	habríais sido
ellos, ellas, ustedes	serían	habrían sido

IMPERATIVO Y MANDATOS (*Imperative and commands*)

(tú)	sé
(usted)	sea
(nosotros)	seamos
(vosotros)	sed
(ustedes)	sean

SUBJUNTIVO (*Subjunctive*)

	PRESENTE (*Present*)	IMPERFECTO (*Imperfect*)	
yo	sea	fuera	fuese
tú	seas	fueras	fueses
él, ella, usted	sea	fuera	fuese
nosotros	seamos	fuéramos	fuésemos
vosotros	seáis	fuerais	fueseis
ellos, ellas, ustedes	sean	fueran	fuesen

	PERFECTO (*Present perfect*)	PLUSCUAMPERFECTO (*Pluperfect*)
yo	haya sido	hubiera, hubiese sido
tú	hayas sido	hubieras, hubieses sido
él, ella, usted	haya sido	hubiera, hubiese sido
nosotros	hayamos sido	hubiéramos, hubiésemos sido
vosotros	hayáis sido	hubierais, hubieseis sido
ellos, ellas, ustedes	hayan sido	hubieran, hubiesen sido

INFINITIVO (*Infinitive*)

    PRESENTE: **ser**   PRETÉRITO (*Perfect*): **haber sido**

GERUNDIO

PRESENTE (*Present participle*):	**siendo**
PRETÉRITO (*Perfect participle*):	**habiendo sido**

PARTICIPIO PASIVO (*Past participle*):   **sido**

23 <u>ser y estar</u>

Ser and **estar** both mean *to be*. Each verb has definite uses, however, and they are not interchangeable.

23.1 Uses of **estar**

A. With an adjective to express a relatively temporary state or condition of the subject.

Estoy muy **cansado.**   Juan **está borracho.**
La sopa **estaba** muy **rica.**   María **estuvo enferma.**

B. To indicate a place or location (but not origin).

¿Dónde está tu amigo?   Madrid **está en España.**
Ellos **están de vacaciones.**   El lápiz **está sobre la mesa.**

C. To indicate the position of a person.

Estamos de pie.   Los niños **están acostados.**

D. With the present participle to form the progressive tenses. (See also *El gerundio ye el participio activo 42.*)

Estuvo estudiando todo el día.
Estábamos hablando cuando entró mi padre.
No hablen de estas cosas cuando **estamos comiendo.**

E. With the past participle to show the result of an action.

Estas cartas **están** muy bien **escritas.**
La ventana **estaba abierta.**

F. To express an opinion.

Estoy contra el uso de la bomba atómica.

G.   With the preposition **para** + infinitive to express the English *to be about to* + infinitive.

Estaban para ir de compras cuando empezó a llover.

H.   With the past participle **muerto**.

El hombre **está muerto**.

I.   Note: Frequently verbs like **verse, hallarse, quedar, encontrarse** are used instead of **estar**.

¿Dónde **queda** este hotel?
Where is this hotel?

A veces **me encuentro (me hallo)** sin palabras.
Sometimes I am speechless (I find myself without words).

Se vio obligado a decírselo.
He (she) felt he (she) had to tell him (her).

23.2 Uses of ser

A.   With an adjective to express an inherent or relatively permanent quality of the subject.

Manuela **es guapa**.	La tiza **es blanca**.
Somos pobres.	Es una casa **antigua**.

B.   With a predicate noun or pronoun.

¿Quién es?   **Es mi amiga Teresa**.
Miguel de Unamuno **es** un escritor famoso.

C.   With occupations, religions, nationalities, and political affiliations.

Él **es abogado**.	Ella **es judía**.
Isabel **es católica**.	Manuela **es española**.
Mi padre **es demócrata**.	Ángela **es comunista**.

D.   With the preposition **de** to express origin, possession, or material from which an object is made.

¿De dónde es Pablo?	**Es de México**.
Las paredes **son de piedra**.	Mi reloj **es de oro**.
¿De quién es este anillo?	**Era de mi madre**; ahora es mío.

E.   With the preposition **para** to indicate the destination of the subject.

Este libro **es para ti**.
Mis ahorros **son para un coche nuevo.**

F.   To express the hour of the day.

¿Qué hora es?   Son las cuatro y media.   Eran[1] **las tres.**

G.   In impersonal expressions.

Es temprano.   **Es mentira.**   **Es lástima.**
Es importante.   **Es evidente.**   **Es inútil.**

H.   With the past participle to express the passive voice. (See also *La voz pasiva 46.*)

Fue atropellado por un coche.
Este profesor **es estimado** por sus estudiantes.
El artículo **fue escrito** por un periodista inteligente.

23.3 Certain adjectives vary in meaning depending upon whether they are used with **ser** or **estar**.

Jorge **es viejo.**   Jorge **está** muy **viejo.**
George is old.   *George looks very old.*

Esta muchacha **es lista.**   Esta muchacha **está lista.**
This girl is clever (alert).   *This girl is ready.*

El profesor **es aburrido.**   El profesor **está aburrido.**
The professor is boring.   *The professor is bored.*

Homero **era ciego.**   Ramón **estaba ciego de rabia.**
Homer was blind.   *Ramón was blind with anger.*

Ricardo **es vivo.**   Ricardo **está vivo.**
Ricardo is clever (alert).   *Ricardo is alive.*

Tu amigo **es atento.**   El estudiante **está atento.**
Your friend is courteous.   *The student pays attention.*

La fruta **es buena** para la salud.   La fruta **está buena** hoy.
Fruit is good for the health.   *The fruit tastes good today.*

---

1. Only the imperfect tense can be used to tell past time.

24 El verbo <u>haber</u> (to have)

INDICATIVO (*Indicative*)

	PRESENTE (*Present*)	IMPERFECTO (*Imperfect*)	PRETÉRITO (*Preterit*)	FUTURO (*Future*)
yo	he	había	hube	habré
tú	has	habías	hubiste	habrás
él, ella, usted	ha (hay[1])	había	hubo	habrá
nosotros	hemos	habíamos	hubimos	habremos
vosotros	habéis	habíais	hubisteis	habréis
ellos, ellas, ustedes	han	habían	hubieron	habrán

	PERFECTO (*Present perfect*)	PLUSCUAMPERFECTO (*Pluperfect*)
yo	he habido	había habido
tú	has habido	habías habido
él, ella, usted	ha habido	había habido
nosotros	hemos habido	habíamos habido
vosotros	habéis habido	habíais habido
ellos, ellas, ustedes	han habido	habían habido

	PRETÉRITO ANTERIOR (*Preterit perfect*)	FUTURO PERFECTO (*Future perfect*)
yo	hube habido	habré habido
tú	hubiste habido	habrás habido
él, ella, usted	hubo habido	habrá habido
nosotros	hubimos habido	habremos habido
vosotros	hubisteis habido	habréis habido
ellos, ellas, ustedes	hubieron habido	habrán habido

---

1. Impersonal form

CONDICIONAL (*Conditional*)

	SIMPLE	PERFECTO (*Conditional perfect*)
yo	habría	habría habido
tú	habrías	habrías habido
él, ella, usted	habría	habría habido
nosotros	habríamos	habríamos habido
vosotros	habríais	habríais habido
ellos, ellas, ustedes	habrían	habrían habido

SUBJUNTIVO (*Subjunctive*)

	PRESENTE (*Present*)	IMPERFECTO (*Imperfect*)	
yo	haya	hubiera	hubiese
tú	hayas	hubieras	hubieses
él, ella, usted	haya	hubiera	hubiese
nosotros	hayamos	hubiéramos	hubiésemos
vosotros	hayáis	hubierais	hubieseis
ellos, ellas, ustedes	hayan	hubieran	hubiesen

	PERFECTO (*Present perfect*)	PLUSCUAMPERFECTO (*Pluperfect*)
yo	haya habido	hubiera, hubiese habido
tú	hayas habido	hubieras, hubieses habido
él, ella, usted	haya habido	hubiera, hubiese habido
nosotros	hayamos habido	hubiéramos, hubiésemos habido
vosotros	hayáis habido	hubierais, hubieseis habido
ellos, ellas, ustedes	hayan habido	hubieran, hubiesen habido

INFINITIVO (*Infinitive*)

PRESENTE: haber   PRETÉRITO (*Perfect*): haber habido

GERUNDIO

PRESENTE (*Present participle*):   habiendo
PRETÉRITO (*Perfect participle*):   habiendo habido

PARTICIPIO PASIVO (*Past participle*):   habido

24.1 Los usos de **haber** (Uses of **haber**)

A. **Haber** is the auxiliary verb used to form all the compound tenses in Spanish. To form these compound tenses, combine the simple tenses of **haber** with the past participle of the verb to be conjugated.

Note: **Tener** (*to have*) is never used as an auxiliary verb. It expresses the meaning *to hold, to possess.* (See *El verbo* **tener** *56*).

B. **hay**

The present tense form **hay** (*there is, there are*) is used impersonally.

Hay mucha gente en el cine.
Hay mucho lodo en la calle.
¿Cuántas millas **hay** de Los Ángeles a Madrid?

In all other tenses, the normal third person singular form of **haber** is used.

Había mucha gente en el cine.
Hubo un gran fuego anoche.

C. The impersonal **hay que** (*it is necessary, one must*) is followed by an infinitive. (See also *El verbo* **deber** *55*.)

Hay que decir la verdad.
Hay que saber hacer las cosas.

In all tenses other than the present, the normal third person singular of **haber** is used.

A causa del viento **hubo que cerrar** la ventana.
Habrá que decir la verdad al juez.

D. The infinitive **haber** used after another verb retains its impersonal sense. The main verb is always in the third person singular.

Debe haber peces en ese lago.
There must be fish in that lake.

Va a haber una tormenta esta noche.
There will be a storm tonight.

Tiene que haber algún motivo para que actúe de tal forma.
There must be a reason why he (she) acts that way.

E.   **Haber de** + infinitive may be conjugated in every person. It expresses a mild future obligation, an expectation, or a commitment. (See also *El verbo* **deber** *55.*)

He de llegar temprano.
I have to arrive early.

Hemos de vernos esta noche.
We have to see each other tonight.

Habían de llegar a las tres y llegaron a las ocho.
They were supposed to arrive at three and they arrived at eight.

25 Los verbos regulares de la primera conjugación

El verbo **amar** (*to love*)

INDICATIVO (*Indicative*)

	PRESENTE (*Present*)	IMPERFECTO (*Imperfect*)	PRETÉRITO (*Preterit*)	FUTURO (*Future*)
yo	amo	amaba	amé	amaré
tú	amas	amabas	amaste	amarás
él, ella, usted	ama	amaba	amó	amará
nosotros	amamos	amábamos	amamos	amaremos
vosotros	amáis	amabais	amasteis	amaréis
ellos, ellas, ustedes	aman	amaban	amaron	amarán

	PERFECTO (*Present perfect*)	PLUSCUAMPERFECTO (*Pluperfect*)
yo	he amado	había amado
tú	has amado	habías amado
él, ella, usted	ha amado	había amado
nosotros	hemos amado	habíamos amado
vosotros	habéis amado	habíais amado
ellos, ellas, ustedes	han amado	habían amado

	PRETÉRITO ANTERIOR (*Preterit perfect*)	FUTURO PERFECTO (*Future perfect*)
yo	hube amado	habré amado
tú	hubiste amado	habrás amado
él, ella, usted	hubo amado	habrá amado
nosotros	hubimos amado	habremos amado
vosotros	hubisteis amado	habréis amado
ellos, ellas, ustedes	hubieron amado	habrán amado

CONDICIONAL (*Conditional*)

	SIMPLE	PERFECTO (*Conditional perfect*)
yo	amaría	habría amado
tú	amarías	habrías amado
él, ella, usted	amaría	habría amado
nosotros	amaríamos	habríamos amado
vosotros	amaríais	habríais amado
ellos, ellas, ustedes	amarían	habrían amado

IMPERATIVO Y MANDATOS (*Imperative and commands*)

(tú)	ama
(usted)	ame
(nosotros)	amemos
(vosotros)	amad
(ustedes)	amen

SUBJUNTIVO (*Subjunctive*)

	PRESENTE (*Present*)	IMPERFECTO (*Imperfect*)	
yo	ame	amara	amase
tú	ames	amaras	amases
él, ella, usted	ame	amara	amase
nosotros	amemos	amáramos	amásemos
vosotros	améis	amarais	amaseis
ellos, ellas, ustedes	amen	amaran	amasen

	PERFECTO (*Present perfect*)	PLUSCUAMPERFECTO (*Pluperfect*)
yo	haya amado	hubiera, hubiese amado
tú	hayas amado	hubieras, hubieses amado
él, ella, usted	haya amado	hubiera, hubiese amado
nosotros	hayamos amado	hubiéramos, hubiésemos amado
vosotros	hayáis amado	hubierais, hubieseis amado
ellos, ellas, ustedes	hayan amado	hubieran, hubiesen amado

INFINITIVO (*Infinitive*)

PRESENTE: **amar**   PRETÉRITO (*Perfect*): **haber amado**

GERUNDIO

    PRESENTE (*Present participle*):   **amando**
    PRETÉRITO (*Perfect participle*): **habiendo amado**

PARTICIPIO PASIVO (*Past participle*): **amado**

26 Los verbos regulares de la segunda conjugación

El verbo **comer** (*to eat*)

INDICATIVO (*Indicative*)

	PRESENTE (*Present*)	IMPERFECTO (*Imperfect*)	PRETÉRITO (*Preterit*)	FUTURO (*Future*)
yo	como	comía	comí	comeré
tú	comes	comías	comiste	comerás
él, ella, usted	come	comía	comió	comerá
nosotros	comemos	comíamos	comimos	comeremos
vosotros	coméis	comíais	comisteis	comeréis
ellos, ellas, ustedes	comen	comían	comieron	comerán

	PERFECTO (*Present perfect*)	PLUSCUAMPERFECTO (*Pluperfect*)
yo	he comido	había comido
tú	has comido	habías comido
él, ella, usted	ha comido	había comido
nosotros	hemos comido	habíamos comido
vosotros	habéis comido	habíais comido
ellos, ellas, ustedes	han comido	habían comido

	PRETÉRITO ANTERIOR (*Preterit perfect*)	FUTURO PERFECTO (*Future perfect*)
yo	hube comido	habré comido
tú	hubiste comido	habrás comido
él, ella, usted	hubo comido	habrá comido
nosotros	hubimos comido	habremos comido
vosotros	hubisteis comido	habréis comido
ellos, ellas, ustedes	hubieron comido	habrán comido

CONDICIONAL (*Conditional*)

	SIMPLE	PERFECTO (*Conditional perfect*)
yo	comería	**habría comido**
tú	comerías	**habrías comido**
él, ella, usted	comería	**habría comido**
nosotros	comeríamos	**habríamos comido**
vosotros	comeríais	**habríais comido**
ellos, ellas, ustedes	comerían	**habrían comido**

IMPERATIVO Y MANDATOS (*Imperative and commands*)

(tú)	com**e**
(usted)	com**a**
(nosotros)	com**amos**
(vosotros)	com**ed**
(ustedes)	com**an**

SUBJUNTIVO (*Subjunctive*)

	PRESENTE (*Present*)	IMPERFECTO (*Imperfect*)	
yo	com**a**	com**iera**	com**iese**
tú	com**as**	com**ieras**	com**ieses**
él, ella, usted	com**a**	com**iera**	com**iese**
nosotros	com**amos**	com**iéramos**	com**iésemos**
vosotros	com**áis**	com**ierais**	com**ieseis**
ellos, ellas, ustedes	com**an**	com**ieran**	com**iesen**

	PERFECTO (*Present perfect*)	PLUSCUAMPERFECTO (*Pluperfect*)
yo	**haya comido**	**hubiera, hubiese comido**
tú	**hayas comido**	**hubieras, hubieses comido**
él, ella, usted	**haya comido**	**hubiera, hubiese comido**
nosotros	**hayamos comido**	**hubiéramos, hubiésemos comido**
vosotros	**hayáis comido**	**hubierais, hubieseis comido**
ellos, ellas, ustedes	**hayan comido**	**hubieran, hubiesen comido**

INFINITIVO (*Infinitive*)

PRESENTE: **comer**   PRETÉRITO (*Perfect*): **haber comido**

GERUNDIO

    PRESENTE (*Present participle*):   **comiendo**
    PRETÉRITO (*Perfect participle*):   **habiendo comido**

PARTICIPIO PASIVO (*Past participle*):   **comido**

27 Los verbos regulares de la tercera conjugación

El verbo **vivir** (*to live*)

INDICATIVO (*Indicative*)

	PRESENTE (*Present*)	IMPERFECTO (*Imperfect*)	PRETÉRITO (*Preterit*)	FUTURO (*Future*)
yo	vivo	vivía	viví	viviré
tú	vives	vivías	viviste	vivirás
él, ella, usted	vive	vivía	vivió	vivirá
nosotros	vivimos	vivíamos	vivimos	viviremos
vosotros	vivís	vivíais	vivisteis	viviréis
ellos, ellas, ustedes	viven	vivían	vivieron	vivirán

	PERFECTO (*Present perfect*)	PLUSCUAMPERFECTO (*Pluperfect*)
yo	he vivido	había vivido
tú	has vivido	habías vivido
él, ella, usted	ha vivido	había vivido
nosotros	hemos vivido	habíamos vivido
vosotros	habéis vivido	habíais vivido
ellos, ellas, ustedes	han vivido	habían vivido

	PRETÉRITO ANTERIOR (*Preterit perfect*)	FUTURO PERFECTO (*Future perfect*)
yo	hube vivido	habré vivido
tú	hubiste vivido	habrás vivido
él, ella, usted	hubo vivido	habrá vivido
nosotros	hubimos vivido	habremos vivido
vosotros	hubisteis vivido	habréis vivido
ellos, ellas, ustedes	hubieron vivido	habrán vivido

CONDICIONAL (*Conditional*)

	SIMPLE	PERFECTO (*Conditional perfect*)
yo	viviría	habría vivido
tú	vivirías	habrías vivido
él, ella, usted	viviría	habría vivido
nosotros	viviríamos	habríamos vivido
vosotros	viviríais	habríais vivido
ellos, ellas, ustedes	vivirían	habrían vivido

IMPERATIVO Y MANDATOS (*Imperative and commands*)

(tú)	vive
(usted)	viva
(nosotros)	vivamos
(vosotros)	vivid
(ustedes)	vivan

SUBJUNTIVO (*Subjunctive*)

	PRESENTE (*Present*)	IMPERFECTO (*Imperfect*)	
yo	viva	viviera	viviese
tú	vivas	vivieras	vivieses
él, ella, usted	viva	viviera	viviese
nosotros	vivamos	viviéramos	viviésemos
vosotros	viváis	vivierais	vivieseis
ellos, ellas, ustedes	vivan	vivieran	viviesen

	PERFECTO (*Present perfect*)	PLUSCUAMPERFECTO (*Pluperfect*)
yo	haya vivido	hubiera, hubiese vivido
tú	hayas vivido	hubieras, hubieses vivido
él, ella, usted	haya vivido	hubiera, hubiese vivido
nosotros	hayamos vivido	hubiéramos, hubiésemos vivido
vosotros	hayáis vivido	hubierais, hubieseis vivido
ellos, ellas, ustedes	hayan vivido	hubieran, hubiesen vivido

INFINITIVO (*Infinitive*)

PRESENTE: vivir   PRETÉRITO (*Perfect*):   haber vivido

GERUNDIO

    PRESENTE (*Present participle*):   **viviendo**
    PRETÉRITO (*Perfect participle*):   **habiendo vivido**

PARTICIPIO PASIVO (*Past participle*):   **vivido**

Tabla de las terminaciones
28 de los verbos regulares

LOS TIEMPOS SIMPLES (*Simple tenses*)

	amar	comer	vivir

PRESENT INDICATIVE

yo	amo	como	vivo
tú	amas	comes	vives
él, ella, usted	ama	come	vive
nosotros	amamos	comemos	vivimos
vosotros	amáis	coméis	vivís
ellos, ellas, ustedes	aman	comen	viven

IMPERFECT INDICATIVE

yo	amaba	comía	vivía
tú	amabas	comías	vivías
él, ella, usted	amaba	comía	vivía
nosotros	amábamos	comíamos	vivíamos
vosotros	amabais	comíais	vivíais
ellos, ellas, ustedes	amaban	comían	vivían

PRETERIT INDICATIVE

yo	amé	comí	viví
tú	amaste	comiste	viviste
él, ella, usted	amó	comió	vivió
nosotros	amamos	comimos	vivimos
vosotros	amasteis	comisteis	vivisteis
ellos, ellas, ustedes	amaron	comieron	vivieron

	amar	comer	vivir

FUTURE INDICATIVE

	amar	comer	vivir
yo	amaré	comeré	viviré
tú	amarás	comerás	vivirás
él, ella, usted	amará	comerá	vivirá
nosotros	amaremos	comeremos	viviremos
vosotros	amaréis	comeréis	viviréis
ellos, ellas, ustedes	amarán	comerán	vivirán

CONDITIONAL

	amar	comer	vivir
yo	amaría	comería	viviría
tú	amarías	comerías	vivirías
él, ella, usted	amaría	comería	viviría
nosotros	amaríamos	comeríamos	viviríamos
vosotros	amaríais	comeríais	viviríais
ellos, ellas, ustedes	amarían	comerían	vivirían

IMPERATIVE AND COMMANDS

	amar	comer	vivir
tú	ama	come	vive
usted	ame	coma	viva
nosotros	amemos	comamos	vivamos
vosotros	amad	comed	vivid
ustedes	amen	coman	vivan

PRESENT PARTICIPLE

	amar	comer	vivir
	amando	comiendo	viviendo

PAST PARTICIPLE

	amar	comer	vivir
	amado	comido	vivido

PRESENT SUBJUNCTIVE

	amar	comer	vivir
yo	ame	coma	viva
tú	ames	comas	vivas
él, ella, usted	ame	coma	viva
nosotros	amemos	comamos	vivamos
vosotros	améis	comáis	viváis
ellos, ellas, ustedes	amen	coman	vivan

	amar	comer	vivir

IMPERFECT SUBJUNCTIVE: -ra ending

	amar	comer	vivir
yo	amara	comiera	viviera
tú	amaras	comieras	vivieras
él, ella, usted	amara	comiera	viviera
nosotros	amáramos	comiéramos	viviéramos
vosotros	amarais	comierais	vivierais
ellos, ellas, ustedes	amaran	comieran	vivieran

IMPERFECT SUBJUNCTIVE: -se ending

	amar	comer	vivir
yo	amase	comiese	viviese
tú	amases	comieses	vivieses
él, ella, usted	amase	comiese	viviese
nosotros	amásemos	comiésemos	viviésemos
vosotros	amaseis	comieseis	vivieseis
ellos, ellas, ustedes	amasen	comiesen	viviesen

29 Los verbos regulares con cambios ortográficos

29.1 Verbs of the first conjugation ending in **-car** change **c** to **qu** before **e**.

	PRETÉRITO	PRESENTE DE SUBJUNTIVO	
buscar:	bus**que**	bus**que**	bus**que**mos
		bus**que**s	bus**qué**is
		bus**que**	bus**que**n

29.2 Verbs of the first conjugation ending in **-gar** change **g** to **gu** before **e**.

	PRETÉRITO	PRESENTE DE SUBJUNTIVO	
llegar:	lle**gué**	lle**gue**	lle**gue**mos
		lle**gue**s	lle**gué**is
		lle**gue**	lle**gue**n

29.3 Verbs of the first conjugation ending in **-zar** change **z** to **c** before **e**.

	PRETÉRITO	PRESENTE DE SUBJUNTIVO	
gozar:	go**cé**	go**ce**	go**ce**mos
		go**ce**s	go**cé**is
		go**ce**	go**ce**n

29.4 Verbs of the first conjugation ending in **-guar** change **gu** to **gü** before **e**.

	PRETÉRITO	PRESENTE DE SUBJUNTIVO	
averiguar:	averi**güé**	averi**güe**	averi**güe**mos
		averi**güe**s	averi**güé**is
		averi**güe**	averi**güe**n

29.5 Verbs of the second and third conjugations ending in **-ger** or **-gir** change **g** to **j** before **o** and **a**.

		PRESENTE DE INDICATIVO	PRESENTE DE SUBJUNTIVO	
recoger:	recojo	recoja	recojamos
		recojas	recojáis
		recoja	recojan
exigir:	exijo	exija	exijamos
		exijas	exijáis
		exija	exijan

29.6 Verbs of the second and third conjugations ending in **-cer** or **-cir** when preceded by a consonant change **c** to **z** before **o** and **a**.

		PRESENTE DE INDICATIVO	PRESENTE DE SUBJUNTIVO	
ejercer:	ejerzo	ejerza	ejerzamos
		ejerzas	ejerzáis
		ejerza	ejerzan
fruncir:	frunzo	frunza	frunzamos
		frunzas	frunzáis
		frunza	frunzan

29.7 Verbs of the third conjugation ending in **-guir** change **gu** to **g** before **o** and **a**.

		PRESENTE DE INDICATIVO	PRESENTE DE SUBJUNTIVO	
distinguir:	distingo	distinga	distingamos
		distingas	distingáis
		distinga	distingan

29.8 Delinquir, the only verb of the third conjugation ending in **-quir**, changes **qu** to **c** before **o** and **a**.

		PRESENTE DE INDICATIVO	PRESENTE DE SUBJUNTIVO	
delinquir:	delinco	delinca	delincamos
		delincas	delincáis
		delinca	delincan

29.9 Verbs of the second conjugation ending in **-eer** change the unstressed **i** to **y** between vowels.

	PRETÉRITO	GERUNDIO	IMPERFECTO DE SUBJUNTIVO	
leer:	leí	leyendo	leyera	leyese
	leíste		leyeras	leyeses
	leyó		leyera	leyese
	leímos		leyéramos	leyésemos
	leísteis		leyerais	leyeseis
	leyeron		leyeran	leyesen

29.10 Verbs of the first conjugation ending in **-iar** or **-uar** change **i** to **í** and **u** to **ú** in all singular forms and in the third person plural of the present indicative and subjunctive, and in the imperative singular.

	PRESENTE DE INDICATIVO		PRESENTE DE SUBJUNTIVO	
enviar:	envío	enviamos	envíe	enviemos
	envías	enviáis	envíes	enviéis
	envía	envían	envíe	envíen
continuar:	continúo	continuamos	continúe	continuemos
	continúas	continuáis	continúes	continuéis
	continúa	continúan	continúe	continúen

Like enviar: variar, espiar, fiar, extraviar, guiar, vaciar, criar, confiar, porfiar

Like continuar: atenuar, extenuar, graduar, exceptuar, acentuar

30 El presente de indicativo

30.1 La formación (Formation)

A. For the three regular conjugations, the present indicative is formed by dropping the infinitive ending (**-ar, -er, -ir**) and adding the present indicative ending for each conjugation.

	amar	comer	vivir
yo	amo	como	vivo
tú	amas	comes	vives
él, ella, usted	ama	come	vive
nosotros	amamos	comemos	vivimos
vosotros	amáis	coméis	vivís
ellos, ellas, ustedes	aman	comen	viven

B. A number of irregular verbs have regular forms in the present indicative, except in the first person singular.

caber	quepo	saber	sé
caer	caigo	salir	salgo
dar	doy	traer	traigo
estar	estoy	valer	valgo
hacer	hago	ver	veo
poner	pongo		

C. Some regular verbs have orthographical changes in the first person singular of the present indicative. (See *Los verbos regulares con cambios ortográficos 29.*)

distinguir	distingo	exigir	exijo
ejercer	ejerzo	recoger	recojo

D. Many verbs have radical (stem) changes in the present indicative in addition to other tenses. (See *Tablas de los verbos con cambios en la raíz 58.*)

sentir: **siento, sientes, siente**, sentimos, sentís, **sienten**
pedir: **pido, pides, pide**, pedimos, pedís, **piden**
pensar: **pienso, piensas, piensa**, pensamos, pensáis, **piensan**
contar: **cuento, cuentas, cuenta**, contamos, contáis, **cuentan**

30.2 El uso (Use)

A. The present indicative is used to express an action that is taking place in the present time, an action actually in progress, or an emphatic statement.

Trabajo demasiado.   *I work too much.*
I am working too much.
I do work too much.

B. The present indicative expresses habitual or constant actions or situations.

Voy a la iglesia los domingos.
La tierra **gira** alrededor del sol.
Los hombres **son** mortales.

C. The present indicative is used in **hace ... que** and **desde hace** constructions. (See these words in the Index.)

D. The present indicative may indicate future action.

Salgo esta noche.   *I'm going out tonight.*
Te **veo** mañana.   *I'll see you tomorrow.*
Mañana **me marcho** para México.   *Tomorrow I'm leaving for Mexico.*

E. The historical present may be used to make a narrative more vivid.

En 1519 Hernán Cortés **ocupa** la capital de los valientes aztecas, y **echa** así los cimientos del futuro México.

31 El imperfecto de indicativo

31.1 La formación (Formation)

A. For the three regular conjugations, the imperfect indicative is formed by dropping the infinitive ending (**-ar**, **-er**, **-ir**) and adding the imperfect indicative endings for each conjugation. The endings for the second and third conjugations are the same.

	amar	comer	vivir
yo	amaba	comía	vivía
tú	amabas	comías	vivías
él, ella, usted	amaba	comía	vivía
nosotros	amábamos	comíamos	vivíamos
vosotros	amabais	comíais	vivíais
ellos, ellas, ustedes	amaban	comían	vivían

B. All verbs in Spanish have regular forms in the imperfect indicative except three.

	ser	ir	ver
yo	era	iba	veía
tú	eras	ibas	veías
él, ella, usted	era	iba	veía
nosotros	éramos	íbamos	veíamos
vosotros	erais	ibais	veíais
ellos, ellas, ustedes	eran	iban	veían

31.2 El uso (Use)

There are several tenses in Spanish which express past time. Besides the general role of expressing the past, each of these tenses has specific functions. The imperfect is used:

A.   To describe repeated or habitual actions in the past. In English, this use is generally expressed by *used to* or a progressive construction. These actions are visualized as continuing over a period of time.

Mi hermana **iba** al cine todas las noches.
My sister used to go to the movies every night.

Él **fumaba** mucho cuando era joven.
He used to smoke a lot when he was young.

Cuando vivía en Nueva York, **iba** mucho a teatro.
When I (he, she, you) lived in New York, I (he, she, you) used to go to the theatre a lot.

B.   To describe physical, mental, or emotional states in the past.

Mi amigo **estaba** enfermo y le **dolía** mucho la cabeza.
My friend was sick and his head ached a lot.

Era alta y delgada pero no **tenía** gracia.
She was tall and slender but had no charm.

C.   To describe weather conditions or nature.

Hacía frío.
El sol **brillaba** y **llovía** al mismo tiempo.

D.   To describe an action that was going on at the time another action took place.

Cuando llegué, ellos **comían**.

E.   To express the time of day.

Eran las dos en punto.

F.   In **hacía** . . . **que** constructions. (See the Index.)

G.   To replace the present. (See *El estilo indirecto 45.*)

32 El pretérito de indicativo

32.1 La formación (Formation)

A. For the three regular conjugations, the preterit indicative is formed by dropping the infinitive ending (-ar, -er, -ir) and adding the preterit indicative endings for each conjugation.

	amar	comer	vivir
yo	amé	comí	viví
tú	amaste	comiste	viviste
él, ella, usted	amó	comió	vivió
nosotros	amamos	comimos	vivimos
vosotros	amasteis	comisteis	vivisteis
ellos, ellas, ustedes	amaron	comieron	vivieron

B. Many irregular verbs have a different set of irregular endings in the preterit. (See also *Tablas de los verbos irregulares 59.*)

-e	-imos
-iste	-isteis
-o	-ieron (-eron after j, ñ, y)

INFINITIVE	IRREGULAR PRETERIT STEM	
andar	anduv-	anduve, anduviste, anduvo, anduvimos, anduvisteis, anduvieron
caber	cup-	cupe, cupiste, cupo, cupimos, cupisteis, cupieron
conducir (verbs ending in -ducir)	conduj-	conduje, condujiste, condujo, condujimos, condujisteis, condujeron
decir	dij-	dije, dijiste, dijo, dijimos, dijisteis, dijeron
estar	estuv-	estuve, estuviste, estuvo, estuvimos, estuvisteis, estuvieron

haber	hub-	hube, hubiste, hubo, hubimos, hubisteis, hubieron
hacer	hic-, hiz-	hice, hiciste, hizo, hicimos, hicisteis, hicieron
poder	pud-	pude, pudiste, pudo, pudimos, pudisteis, pudieron
poner	pus-	puse, pusiste, puso, pusimos, pusisteis, pusieron
querer	quis-	quise, quisiste, quiso, quisimos, quisisteis, quisieron
saber	sup-	supe, supiste, supo, supimos, supisteis, supieron
tener	tuv-	tuve, tuviste, tuvo, tuvimos, tuvisteis, tuvieron
traer	traj-	traje, trajiste, trajo, trajimos, trajisteis, trajeron
venir	vin-	vine, viniste, vino, vinimos, vinisteis, vinieron

C.   Completely irregular in the preterit are:

	dar	ir	ser
yo	di	fui	fui
tú	diste	fuiste	fuiste
él, ella, usted	dio	fue	fue
nosotros	dimos	fuimos	fuimos
vosotros	disteis	fuisteis	fuisteis
ellos, ellas, ustedes	dieron	fueron	fueron

32.2 El uso (Use)

The preterit is used to relate a completed past event or a sudden and momentary occurrence in the past. The time limit is expressed or implied by the context. The emphasis of the preterit is narrative, whereas the imperfect is mainly descriptive.

Ayer **tomé** el autobús.
Yesterday I took the bus.

Juan **terminó** su tarea.
Juan finished his homework.

Estudiaron mucho para los exámenes.
They (you) studied a lot for the exams.

Mi padre no me **prestó** su coche.
My father didn't lend me his car.

Tuvimos que trabajar durante las vacaciones.
We had to work during vacation.

María **salió** sin despedirse.
Maria went out without saying good-bye.

¿**Recibieron** muchos regalos?
Did they (you) receive a lot of gifts?

La semana pasada **fuimos** al teatro.
Last week we went to the theatre.

Se pasó la vida trabajando.
He (she, you) spent his (her, your) life working.

Gastaron mucho dinero en este viaje.
They (you) spent a lot of money on this trip.

32.3 El contraste entre el pretérito y el imperfecto (Preterit versus imperfect)

A. Although verbs denoting mental activity such as **conocer**, **saber**, **querer**, and **poder** are expressed by the imperfect tense in most cases, they have a special meaning when used in the preterit.

¿**Conocía** usted a mi prima?   *Did you know my cousin?*
La **conocí** ayer.   *I met her yesterday.*

Sabían la verdad.   *They knew the truth.*
Supieron la verdad.   *They found out the truth.*

Quería hablar con ellos.   *I wanted to talk to them.*
Quise hablar con ellos.   *I tried to talk to them.*

No **podía** venir.   *He (she) wasn't able to come.*
No **pudo** venir.   *He (she) couldn't (refused to) come.*

B. The following story based on the opera *Carmen* illustrates the use of the preterit and the imperfect.

Caminando por una plaza de Sevilla, en la que se **encontraban** situados la Fábrica de Tabacos y también el cuartel militar, Carmen la cigarrera **conoció** a Don José que **era** un sargento de la guarnición. Ella **trató** de conquistarle arrojándole una flor, pero no lo **consiguió**. Más tarde Carmen se **peleó** con una compañera y la **apuñaló**. La **arrestaron**, pero Don José, que ya se había enamorado de ella, la **dejó** escapar y se **constituyó** él mismo en prisión. Carmen **necesitaba** ganarse la vida y **aceptó** un trabajo por las noches en una taberna que **servía** de punto de reunión a toreros, ladrones y soldados. En esta taberna ella **cantaba** y **bailaba** con mucha gracia y salero. Cuando Don José **salió** de la cárcel, se **enteró** que su superior estaba cortejando a la graciosa gitanilla y, cegado por los celos, **retó** al oficial. Perseguido por la ley y perdida su carrera de militar, Don José no **tuvo** más remedio que escuchar los consejos de Carmen de huir con ella y de reunirse a una banda de contrabandistas que **pertenecían** a la misma tribu de Carmen.

Después de un tiempo, Carmen **acabó** por aburrirse de la dura vida que **llevaba** viviendo en las montañas. **Echaba** de menos la taberna en que **bailaba** y la vida fácil que le **proporcionaba**. Así que cuando se **presentó** la ocasión, **convenció** a Don José de ir a ver a su madre que **estaba** enferma. Ella **regresó** a su baile y a su canto. **Conocía** al famoso torero Escamillo y éste **empezó** a cortejarla. Carmen, deslumbrada por su fama y siendo de corazón voluble, **terminó** por enamorarse de él. No **pasó** mucho tiempo antes de que la historia de lo que **pasaba** llegara a los oídos de Don José. Él **fue** inmediatamente a buscarla y por más que él **prometía** perdonarla y que **insistía** en que regresara a vivir con él, ella se **negó** y le **arrojó** su anillo. Este hecho le **costó** la vida. Don José se **abalanzó** sobre ella y le **hundió** un puñal en el corazón en frente de la salida de la Plaza de Toros de Sevilla. **Cayó** muerta Carmen al momento en que **surgía** Escamillo triunfalmente de la corrida. Loco de dolor, Don José se **dejó** caer sobre el cuerpo de su amada.

32.4 El pasado próximo: **acabar de** + infinitivo (The recent past)

A. The recent past is expressed with the present tense of the verb **acabar** followed by **de** + an infinitive.

Acabo de terminar mi trabajo.
I have just finished my work.

B. A past action that took place immediately before another past action is expressed by the imperfect of **acabar**.

Acababa de salir mi hermano cuando lo llamaron por teléfono.
My brother had just left when someone telephoned him.

33 El participio pasivo y el perfecto de indicativo

33.1 El participio pasivo (Past participle)

A. The past participle of regular verbs is formed by changing the infinitive ending **-ar** to **-ado** and the infinitive endings **-er** and **-ir** to **-ido**.

am~~ar~~	am**ado**	com~~er~~	com**ido**	viv~~ir~~	viv**ido**
habl~~ar~~	habl**ado**	vend~~er~~	vend**ido**	ped~~ir~~	ped**ido**

The past participle is used in compound tenses and as an adjective.

B. The following verbs have irregular past participles.

abrir	**abierto**	imprimir	**impreso**
absolver	**absuelto**	morir	**muerto**
cubrir	**cubierto**	poner	**puesto**
decir	**dicho**	resolver	**resuelto**
disolver	**disuelto**	ver	**visto**
escribir	**escrito**	volver	**vuelto**
hacer	**hecho**		

All compounds of these verbs have the same irregularity, except **bendecir** and **maldecir** (see following list).

C. The following verbs have a regular past participle used in the compound tenses and an irregular past participle used as an adjective.

INFINITIVE	REGULAR PAST PARTICIPLE	IRREGULAR PAST PAST PARTICIPLE
absorber	**absorbido**	**absorto**
abstraer	**abstraído**	**abstracto**
afligir	**afligido**	**aflicto**
asumir	**asumido**	**asunto**
bendecir	**bendecido**	**bendito**

comprender	comprendido	comprenso
concluir	concluido	concluso
confundir	confudido	confuso
contraer	contraído	contracto
convencer	convencido	convicto
convertir	convertido	converso
corregir	corregido	correcto
descalzar	descalzado	descalzo
despertar	despertado	despierto
difundir	difundido	difuso
elegir	elegido	electo
exceptar	exceptado	excepto
excluir	excluido	excluso
expresar	expresado	expreso
expulsar	expulsado	expulso
extender	extendido	extenso
extingir	extingido	extinto
fijar	fijado	fijo
freír	freído	frito
incluir	incluido	incluso
injertar	injertado	injerto
invertir	invertido	inverso
juntar	juntado	junto
maldecir	maldecido	maldito
manifestar	manifestado	manifiesto
nacer	nacido	nato
omitir	omitido	omiso
prender	prendido	preso
prostituir	prostituido	prostituto
proveer	proveído	provisto
recluir	recluido	recluso
romper	rompido[1]	roto
salvar	salvado	salvo
sofreír	sofreído	sofrito
soltar	soltado	suelto
substituir	substituido	substituto
sujetar	sujetado	sujeto
suprimir	suprimido	supreso
suspender	suspendido	suspenso
teñir	teñido	tinto
torcer	torcido	tuerto

1. This form is found only in classical literature. **Roto** is used in its place today.

Note: The irregular past participles **frito, preso, provisto,** and **roto** are also used in compound tenses.

33.2 El perfecto de indicativo (Present perfect indicative)

To form compound tenses in Spanish, combine the simple tenses of **haber,** the auxiliary verb, with the past participle of the verb to be conjugated.

A.   La formación (Formation)

The present perfect is formed with the present tense of **haber** and a past participle.

	amar	comer	vivir
yo	**he amado**	**he comido**	**he vivido**
tú	**has amado**	**has comido**	**has vivido**
él, ella, usted	**ha amado**	**ha comido**	**ha vivido**
nosotros	**hemos amado**	**hemos comido**	**hemos vivido**
vosotros	**habéis amado**	**habéis comido**	**habéis vivido**
ellos, ellas, ustedes	**han amado**	**han comido**	**han vivido**

B.   El uso (Use)

1.   The present perfect tense is used to express an entirely completed past action without reference to a particular time.

Hemos oído la noticia por la televisión.
We heard the news on television.

¿Han comido allí?
Did you eat there?

2.   There is very little difference between the present perfect and the preterit. For all practical purposes, the perfect is used mainly for past events closely related to the present time.

He visto una película francesa que me gusta mucho.
I saw a French film I like very much.

Mis padres me **han regalado** un nuevo reloj para mi cumpleaños.
My parents gave me a new watch for my birthday.

3.   The present perfect is used also to indicate that an action continues into the present.

Mi hermana **ha estado** enferma.
My sister has been sick.

España **ha producido** escritores famosos.
Spain has been producing famous writers.

34 El pluscuamperfecto

34.1 La formación (Formation)

The pluperfect is a compound tense formed with the imperfect of **haber** and a past participle.

yo	**había escrito**
tú	**habías comido**
él, ella, usted	**había leído**
nosotros	**habíamos venido**
vosotros	**habíais dormido**
ellos, ellas, ustedes	**habían llegado**

34.2 El uso (Use)

The pluperfect expresses an action that took place before another action in the past or a condition that existed before another past event.

Ayer mi primo ya **había salido** de casa cuando llegaron sus amigos.
Yesterday my cousin already had left when his friends arrived.

Comimos lo que nos **habían recomendado.**
We ate what they had recommended to us.

Me **habían hablado** mucho de la película que vi anoche.
They had talked to me a lot about the film I saw last night.

Habló mucho de los museos que **había visitado.**
He (she, you) talked a lot about the museums he (she, you) visited.

Si hacía frío es porque **había nevado** toda la noche.
If it was cold it's because it had snowed all night.

35 El pretérito anterior

35.1 La formación (Formation)

The preterit perfect is a compound tense formed with the preterit of **haber** and a past participle.

yo	**hube escrito**
tú	**hubiste comido**
él, ella, usted	**hubo leído**
nosotros	**hubimos venido**
vosotros	**hubisteis dormido**
ellos, ellas, ustedes	**hubieron llegado**

35.2 El uso (Use)

Like the pluperfect, the preterit perfect expresses an action that took place before another action in the past. It is a narrative tense used in literary contexts and very seldom in conversation. It is always preceded by a time expression such as:

apenas	*barely, hardly*
en seguida que	*as soon as*
tan pronto como	*as soon as*
después que	*after*
luego que	*after*
en cuanto	*as soon as*

Tan pronto como hubo salido el sol, me desperté.
As soon as the sun had come up, I woke up.

Después que hubieron estudiado, fueron al cine.
After they had studied, they went to the movies.

36 El futuro

36.1 La formación (Formation)

A. For all three conjugations, the future is formed by adding the following endings to the infinitive.

	amar	comer	vivir
yo	amaré	comeré	viviré
tú	amarás	comerás	vivirás
él, ella, usted	amará	comerá	vivirá
nosotros	amaremos	comeremos	viviremos
vosotros	amaréis	comeréis	viviréis
ellos, ellas, ustedes	amarán	comerán	vivirán

B. Irregular future stems

caber	cabré	querer	querré
decir	diré	saber	sabré
haber	habré	salir	saldré
hacer	haré	tener	tendré
poder	podré	valer	valdré
poner	pondré	venir	vendré

Verbs that are irregular in the future have irregular stems. The same stem is used in all persons. Endings for all verbs, including irregular verbs, are regular.

36.2 El uso (Use)

A. The future tense is used for actions expected to happen in the future.

Mañana me levantaré temprano.	*Tomorrow I'll get up early.*
Esta noche saldremos juntos.	*Tonight we'll go out together.*
¿Vendrás conmigo?	*Will you come with me?*

[132]

B. In Spanish, the future tense is often used to express probability or conjecture concerning an action or a state in the present time.

¿Quién **será**?	*Who can it be?*
Será Juan.	*It must be Juan.*
Tendrá unos veinte años.	*He (she, you) must be about twenty.*
¿**Se atreverá** a negarlo?	*Do you dare to deny it?*
	Does he (she) dare to deny it?

C. The future is used in the result clause of a conditional sentence, and the present tense is used after **si**. (See also *Las cláusulas condicionales 40*.)

Si tengo dinero, **iré** a Europa.
If I have money, I'll go to Europe.

36.3 El futuro cercano: **ir a** + infinitivo (Near future)

The near future is formed with the present tense of the verb **ir** followed by **a** + an infinitive.

Voy a escribir una carta.	*I am going to write a letter.*
Vamos a estudiar toda la noche.	*We are going to study all night.*

37 El futuro perfecto

37.1 La formación (Formation)

The future perfect is a compound tense formed with the future tense of **haber** and a past participle.

yo	**habré escrito**
tú	**habrás comido**
él, ella, usted	**habrá leído**
nosotros	**habremos venido**
vosotros	**habréis dormido**
ellos, ellas, ustedes	**habrán llegado**

37.2 El uso (Use)

The future perfect is used to express an action that will have taken place before another future action.

Habremos terminado esta tarea antes de cenar.
We'll have this homework finished before supper.

¿**Se habrán marchado** para el fin del mes?
Will they have gone by the end of the month?

37.3 The future perfect expresses probability or conjecture concerning a recent action.

Lo **habrán comprado** en Europa.	*They must have bought it in Europe.*
Habrá salido ya.	*He (she) must have left already.*

38 El condicional (El potencial)

38.1 La formación (Formation)

A. For all three conjugations, the conditional is formed by adding the following endings to the infinitive.

	amar	**comer**	**vivir**
yo	amaría	comería	viviría
tú	amarías	comerías	vivirías
él, ella, usted	amaría	comería	viviría
nosotros	amaríamos	comeríamos	viviríamos
vosotros	amaríais	comeríais	viviríais
ellos, ellas, ustedes	amarían	comerían	vivirían

B. Irregular conditional stems

caber	**cabría**	querer	**querría**
decir	**diría**	saber	**sabría**
haber	**habría**	salir	**saldría**
hacer	**haría**	tener	**tendría**
poder	**podría**	valer	**valdría**
poner	**pondría**	venir	**vendría**

Verbs that are irregular in the conditional have irregular stems. The same stems are irregular in the conditional as in the future. For each verb, the same stem is used in all persons. Endings for both regular and irregular verbs are regular.

38.2 El uso (Use)

A. The conditional is the mood used to express actions subject to a condition. (See also *Las cláusulas condicionales 40.*)

[135]

Si tuviera mucho dinero, no **trabajaría**.
If (he, she, you) had a lot of money, I (he, she, you) wouldn't work.

Si pudiera, **iría** contigo.
If I (he, she) could, I (he, she) would go with you.

B.   The conditional is used to express a polite request, statement, or wish.

¿Podría usted esperarme un momento?
Could you wait for me a moment?

Nos gustaría conocer a sus padres.
We would like to know your (his, her, their) parents.

Desearía pedirle un favor.
I'd like to ask you a favor.

C.   The conditional expresses hypothetical statements or questions.

¿Quién lo **creería**?
Who would believe it?

¿Me **haría** usted este favor?
Would you do me this favor?

D.   The conditional is used to indicate actions that were considered future at a particular moment in the past.

Mi tío me dijo que **saldría** temprano.
My uncle told me he would leave early.

Nos avisaron que **llegarían** por avión.
They notified us that they would arrive by plane.

38.3 The conditional expresses probability or conjecture with reference to a past action.

Serían las tres cuando nos llamaron.
It was probably three o'clock when they called us.

¿Quién **sería**?
Who could it have been?   (I wonder who it was?)

39 El perfecto de condicional (potencial)

39.1 La formación (Formation)

The conditional perfect is a compound tense formed with the conditional of
haber and a past participle.

yo	**habría escrito**
tú	**habrías comido**
él, ella, usted	**habría leído**
nosotros	**habríamos venido**
vosotros	**habríais dormido**
ellos, ellas, ustedes	**habrían llegado**

39.2 El uso (Use)

The conditional perfect expresses a condition that was not fulfilled at a given
moment in the past. It is used in the result clause of a conditional sentence,
and the pluperfect subjunctive is used after si. (See also *Las cláusulas
condicionales 40.*)

Si yo hubiera tenido dinero, lo **habría repartido**.
If I had had money, I would have given it out.

In modern Spanish, this tense is used very little and is generally replaced by
the pluperfect subjunctive.

Si yo hubiera tenido dinero, lo **hubiera repartido**.

39.3 The conditional perfect may also express probability or conjecture with
reference to a past action.

¿Qué **habría hecho** ella?
What could she have done?

Habrían olvidado que los invité.
They had probably forgotten I invited them.

40 Las cláusulas condicionales

The most common conditional sentences involve the following sequences of tenses.

CONDITION	RESULT CLAUSE
Si + presente	futuro
Si + imperfecto de subjuntivo	condicional
Si + pluscuamperfecto de subjuntivo	{ perfecto de condicional { pluscuamperfecto de subjuntivo[1]

Si comes mucho, te enfermarás.
If you eat a lot, you'll get sick.

Te enfermarás si comes mucho.[2]
You'll get sick if you eat a lot.

Si fuéramos ricos, estaríamos siempre de viaje.
If we were rich, we would always be traveling.

Estaríamos siempre de viaje si fuéramos ricos.[2]
We would always be traveling if we were rich.

Si tuviera ella teléfono, la llamaría.
If she had a phone, I would call her.

Si hubiéramos comido mucho, nos habríamos enfermado.
Si hubiéramos comido mucho, nos hubiéramos enfermado.[1]
If we had eaten a lot, we would have been sick.

Si hubieran tomado el avión, habrían llegado a tiempo.
Si hubieran tomado el avión, hubieran llegado[1] a tiempo.
If they had taken the plane, they would have arrived on time.

---

1. The conditional perfect is used very little and is often replaced by the pluperfect subjunctive.
2. A si-clause may either precede or follow the result clause.

El imperativo y
41 los mandatos
_____

The imperative has the function of expressing a command or a request.

41.1 Los mandatos: **usted(es)** (Formal commands)

A. Formation

The forms used for the formal command are those of the third person singular and plural of the present subjunctive. (See *El presente de subjuntivo 47.*) **Usted** and **ustedes** are usually expressed with the verb and are placed after it.

amar	comer	vivir
ame usted	**coma** usted	**viva** usted
amen ustedes	**coman** ustedes	**vivan** ustedes

B. The stem for the formal command forms (and for the present subjunctive) is that of the first person singular of the present indicative, except for the five irregular verbs (see C).

INFINITIVE	PRESENT INDICATIVE	FORMAL COMMANDS	
contar	cuento	**cuente** usted	**cuenten** ustedes
perder	pierdo	**pierda** usted	**pierdan** ustedes
poder	puedo	**pueda** usted	**puedan** ustedes
preferir	prefiero	**prefiera** usted	**prefieran** ustedes
dormir	duermo	**duerma** usted	**duerman** ustedes
pedir	pido	**pida** usted	**pidan** ustedes
seguir	sigo	**siga** usted	**sigan** ustedes
caer	caigo[1]	**caiga** usted	**caigan** ustedes

_____

1. Note that all the **-go** endings change to **-ga(n)**.

decir	digo	**diga** usted	**digan** ustedes
hacer	hago	**haga** usted	**hagan** ustedes
oír	oigo	**oiga** usted	**oigan** ustedes
poner	pongo	**ponga** usted	**pongan** ustedes
salir	salgo	**salga** usted	**salgan** ustedes
tener	tengo	**tenga** usted	**tengan** ustedes
traer	traigo	**traiga** usted	**traigan** ustedes
venir	vengo	**venga** usted	**vengan** ustedes
valer	valgo	**valga** usted	**valgan** ustedes
conducir	conduzco	**conduzca** usted	**conduzcan** ustedes
conocer	conozco	**conozca** usted	**conozcan** ustedes
construir	construyo	**construya** usted	**construyan** ustedes
ver	veo	**vea** usted	**vean** ustedes

C.   The following verbs are irregular.

dar	doy	**dé** usted	**den** ustedes
estar	estoy	**esté** usted	**estén** ustedes
ir	voy	**vaya** usted	**vayan** ustedes
saber	sé	**sepa** usted	**sepan** ustedes
ser	soy	**sea** usted	**sean** ustedes

D.   The same forms are used for the formal negative commands.

no **diga** usted	no **digan** ustedes
no **ponga** usted	no **pongan** ustedes
no **salga** usted	no **salgan** ustedes
no **duerma** usted	no **duerman** ustedes
no **traduzca** usted	no **traduzcan** ustedes

41.2 El imperativo: tú y **vosotros** (Familiar commands)

A.   The singular imperative (**tú**) has the same form as the third person singular of the present indicative. The pronoun **tú** is generally not used.

amar	**ama**	dormir	**duerme**
hablar	**habla**	conocer	**conoce**
comer	**come**	pedir	**pide**
aprender	**aprende**	seguir	**sigue**
vivir	**vive**	volver	**vuelve**

B. Irregular imperatives

decir	**di**	salir	**sal**
hacer	**haz**	ser	**sé**
ir	**ve**	tener	**ten**
poner	**pon**	vinir	**ven**

C. The negative familiar singular command is the same as the second person singular of the present subjunctive. It can also be formed by adding -s to the formal command form.

no **cuentes**	no **estés**	no **pongas**	no **sepas**
no **digas**	no **fumes**	no **salgas**	no **sigas**
no **des**	no **pierdas**	no seas	no **vayas**

D. The plural imperative (**vosotros, -as**) is formed by dropping the -**r** of the infinitive and replacing it with -**d**. The pronoun **vosotros** is generally not used.

amar	**amad**	hablar	**hablad**
comer	**comed**	vivir	**vivid**
dormir	**dormid**	salir	**salid**
seguir	**seguid**	venir	**vinid**

E. The negative familiar plural command is the same as the second person plural of the present subjunctive.

amar	no **améis**	perder	no **perdáis**
hablar	no **habléis**	vivir	no **viváis**
comer	no **comáis**	venir	no **vengáis**

Note: In most Spanish-speaking countries, the plural imperative (**vosotros**) is replaced by the formal plural command (**ustedes**).

41.3 El mandato: **nosotros** (First person plural commands: *let's*)

A. The first person plural command has the same form as the first person plural of the present subjunctive. The pronoun **nosotros** is generally not used.

amar	**amemos**	estar	**estemos**
comer	**comamos**	saber	**sepamos**
vivir	**vivamos**	salir	**salgamos**

B. The first person plural command in the affirmative can also be expressed with **vamos a** + infinitive.

Vamos a comer.	*Let's eat.*
Vamos a estudiar.	*Let's study.*
Vamos a ver.	*Let's see.*

Vamos a + **ir** or another verb of motion expresses the near future. (See also *El futuro cercano 36.3*.)

Vamos a ir los dos.	*We are both going to go.*
Vamos a salir mañana.	*We are going to leave tomorrow.*

Vamos + a noun is used for *let's go.*

Vamos al cine.	*Let's go to the movies.*
Vamos a la playa.	*Let's go to the beach.*

The negative first person plural command may be expressed in two ways.

No vayamos a comer.	
No comamos.	*Let's not go to eat.*

No vayamos al cine.	*Let's not go to the movies.*
No vayamos a la playa.	*Let's not go to the beach.*

41.4 The infinitive may be used as an impersonal command.

No **fumar.**	*Smoking is not permitted.*
Favor de **traducir** este pasaje.	*Translate this passage, please.*
No **reunirse** sin permiso.	*No assembling without a permit.*

41.5 La posición de los pronombres personales (Position of object pronouns)

A. Affirmative command

Object and reflexive pronouns follow and are attached to the verb.

Déme usted el libro.	**Démelo** usted.
Pide el permiso a él.	**Pídeslo** a él.
Ponga usted los libros allí.	**Póngalos** usted allí.
Compremos los discos.	**Comprémoslos.**

B.   Negative command

With negative commands, however, object pronouns precede the verb and are placed between the negative word and the verb. (See also *Placement of Personal Pronouns 18.1G.*)

Nunca me digas eso.	**No lo haga** usted.
No los ponga usted allí.	**No me lo digan** ustedes.

42 El gerundio

42.1 La formación (Formation)

A. The present participle of regular verbs is formed by substituting the ending **-ando** for the infinitive ending **-ar**, and the ending **-iendo** for the infinitive endings **-er** and **-ir**. The English equivalent ends in *-ing*.

amar	ama**ndo**	*loving*
comer	comi**endo**	*eating*
vivir	vivi**endo**	*living*

B. The present participle of **-er** and **-ir** verbs with a stem change in the preterit has the same irregularity as the third person plural of the preterit.

pedir	pidieron	**pidiendo**
sentir	sintieron	**sintiendo**
venir	vinieron	**viniendo**
caer	cayeron	**cayendo**
oír	oyeron	**oyendo**
dormir	durmieron	**durmiendo**
poder	pudieron	**pudiendo**
morir	murieron	**muriendo**
vestirse	se vistieron	**vistiéndose**

C. Irregular present participles

decir	**diciendo**
ir	**yendo**

42.2 El uso (Use)

A. The present participle frequently denotes one of two actions which the same person(s) perform(s) simultaneously.

¿Escucha usted la radio **leyendo** su periódico?

[145]

No le gustan los obreros que hablan **trabajando.**
Mis amigos y yo charlamos **esperando** al profesor.
Ella entró **cantando** en la sala.

B.   The present participle is used in absolute clauses placed before or after the main clause.

Hablando se entiende la gente.
By speaking people understand each other.

Estudiando mucho aprenderás francés.
By studying a lot you'll learn French.

No me preocupo **estando** él conmigo.
By his being with me, I will not worry.

Siendo rico, todo se consigue.
By being rich, you can get anything.

C.   The progressive tenses

The present participle used after **estar** and also after **ir**[1], **venir**[1], **quedar, continuar, seguir,** and **andar** expresses an action in progress at a given moment.

Juan **está hablando** con Alicia.
Estaban mirando la televisión cuando se apagaron las luces.
¿Qué **están leyendo** ahora?
Anda diciendo muchas cosas sobre ti.
Iba pensando en sus problemas.
Entró el profesor, pero los alumnos **siguieron hablando.**
La población **continúa creciendo.**

D.   Unlike its English equivalents, the present participle is not used to modify a noun in Spanish.

la clase obrera	*the working class*
un bastón	*a walking cane*
una muñeca que habla	*a talking doll*
una pareja de baile	*a dancing partner*
un naipe	*a playing card*

Exceptions:

agua hirviendo	*boiling water*

---

1. The present participles of the verbs **ir** and **venir** (**yendo** and **viniendo**) are seldom used in the progressive tense.

una casa ardiendo   *a burning house*

E.   The form used as an adjective (also called *present participle* in English)
     or as a noun (called *gerund* in English) is called in Spanish **el participio
     activo**. The endings are **-ante** for **-ar** verbs, and **-iente** or **-ente** for **-er** and
     -ir verbs.

	GERUNDIO	PARTICIPIO ACTIVO
caminar	**caminando**	**caminante**
andar	**andando**	**andante**
amar	**amando**	**amante**
correr	**corriendo**	**corriente**
vivir	**viviendo**	**viviente**
sobresalir	**sobresaliendo**	**sobresaliente**
pretender	**pretendiendo**	**pretendiente**
sorprender	**sorprendiendo**	**sorprendente**
exigir	**exigiendo**	**exigente**

Los **amantes** se pelearon. (*noun*)
The lovers quarreled.

El puesto tuvo muchos **pretendientes**. (*noun*)
The position had many candidates.

Mi jefe es muy **exigente**. (*adjective*)
My boss is very demanding.

Esta casa tiene agua **corriente**. (*adjective*)
This house has running water.

42.3 La posición de los pronombres personales   (Position of object pronouns)

A.   Object and reflexive pronouns follow and are attached to the present
     participle.

Escuchándola, se durmió.
Conociéndolos como los conozco, sé que son incapaces de mentir.

B.   In the progressive tenses, however, object pronouns may be attached to
     the present participle or placed before the verb **estar**. (See also
     Placement of Personal Pronouns 18.1G.)

Lo está estudiando.   or   **Está estudiándolo.**
Las estábamos mirando.   or   **Estábamos mirándolas.**

43 El infinitivo

43.1 Spanish verbs fall into three groups which can be identified by the infinitive ending.

-ar	amar, hablar, comenzar, pensar, contar
-er	comer, conocer, satisfacer, llover, saber
-ir	vivir, prohibir, sufrir, salir, partir

The infinitive expresses the meaning of the verb in a general sense without distinction of person or number.

A. In Spanish, the infinitive is the verbal form that is used after all prepositions. In English, the present participle is generally used.

Se fueron **sin hablar** conmigo.
They left without speaking to me.

El profesor nos obliga **a estudiar.**
The professor forces us to study.

Prepararon la comida **antes de salir.**
They prepared the food before leaving.

B. The preposition is repeated before each infinitive in a series.

Pedro se cansó **de** estudiar, **de** escribir y **de** trabajar.
Los estudiantes aprenden **a** hablar y **a** leer.

C. **Al** + an infinitive is equivalent to the English *upon (on)* + a present participle.

Al salir de casa, notó que empezó a llover.
Upon leaving the house, he noted that it started to rain.

Al entrar en la casa, se quita el sombrero.
Upon entering the house, he removes his hat.

D. In Spanish, when two verbs are used consecutively,[1] the second one is an infinitive, whether or not it is preceded by a preposition.

Pienso salir mañana.
I intend to leave tomorrow.

Nadie **puede entrar** allí.
Nobody may enter there.

Queremos verlos inmediatamente.
We want to see them immediately.

Mandó pintar la casa.
He (she) had the house painted.

Pedro se **cansó de estudiar**.
Pedro got tired of studying.

El tren **tarda en llegar**.
The train is delayed.

E. The infinitive is used instead of the subjunctive when the subject is the same in the main clause and the dependent clause. (See *47.4C*.)

Mis amigos quieren ir al cine.
Prefiero saber la verdad.

F. The infinitive is used after impersonal expressions denoting necessity, obligation, convenience, and so on to convey a general meaning. (See *Las expresiones impersonales y el subjuntivo 52*.)

Es necesario estudiar para los exámenes.
Es imposible viajar sin dinero.
Es preciso levantarse temprano.
Se prohibe fumar en clase.

G. The infinitive is used after **tener que** and **hay que**.

Tengo que salir mañana.
Tuvieron que comer sin apetito.
Tuvimos que viajar con poco dinero.
Hay que tomar el avión a las dos de la tarde.
Hay que regresar a casa sin perder tiempo.

---

1. Other than verbs in compound and progressive tenses.

H.   The infinitive may be used as a noun.

el Cantar de los Cantares   El comer engorda.
the Song of Songs   *Eating makes one fat.*

El prometer no empobrece.   El practicar hace el maestro.
Promises will not make you poor.   *Practice makes perfect.*

Es un decir.
It is a saying.

I.   The perfect infinitive is formed with the infinitive of **haber** and a past
      participle.

haber visitado   *having visited*
haber estudiado   *having studied*

The perfect infinitive expresses an action entirely completed in the
past.

Después de **haber trabajado** muchos años, se retiró.
After he worked (having worked) many years, he retired.

Le expulsaron por **haber llegado** tarde.
They expelled him because he was late (for having arrived late).

43.2 La posición de los pronombres personales (Position of object
pronouns)

Object and reflexive pronouns follow and are generally attached to the
infinitive when they are objects of the infinitive. They may also precede the
conjugated verb. (See also *Placement of Personal Pronouns 18.1G.*)

Debes de pensarlo mucho. ⎫
Lo debes de pensar mucho. ⎭   *You must think about it a lot.*

Tienen que obedecerme. ⎫
Me tienen que obedecer. ⎭   *They have to obey me.*

Queremos dárselos para su boda. ⎫ *We want to give them to him for*
Se los queremos dar para su boda.⎭ *his wedding.*

Hay que trabajar para ganarse la vida.
One must work to earn a living.

43.3 Los verbos usados sin una preposición (Verbs used without a preposition)

Some verbs may be directly followed by an infinitive without a preposition.

Me gusta ir de compras.   *I like to go shopping.*

aceptar	*to accept*
aconsejar	*to advise*
admitir	*to admit*
adorar	*to adore, to love*
bastar	*to be enough, to be sufficient*
buscar	*to look for, to search for*
conseguir	*to obtain, to succeed in*
convenir	*to be fitting, to be advisable*
creer	*to believe, to think*
deber	*to have to, must, ought*
decidir	*to decide*
declarar	*to state, to declare*
dejar	*to let, to allow*
desear	*to wish, to desire*
detestar	*to detest, to hate*
elegir	*to elect*
escoger	*to choose*
escuchar	*to listen*
esperar	*to hope, to expect*
evitar	*to avoid*
faltar	*to lack*
gustarle a uno	*to like*
hacer	*to make*
imaginarse	*to imagine*
impedir	*to prevent*
importar	*to matter, to be important*
intentar	*to try, to attempt*
interesar	*to interest*
lograr	*to succeed in*
mandar	*to order, to command*
merecer	*to deserve, to merit*
mirar	*to look at*
necesitar	*to need*
odiar	*to hate*
oír	*to hear*
olvidar	*to forget*

ordenar	*to order, to command*
parecer	*to appear, to seem*
pedir	*to ask for*
pensar	*to intend, to think, to plan*
permitir	*to permit, to allow, to let*
poder	*to be able, may, can*
preferir	*to prefer*
prohibir	*to prohibit, forbid*
prometer	*to promise*
proponer	*to propose*
pretender	*to claim, to assert*
querer	*to wish, to want*
recomendar	*to recommend*
rehusar	*to refuse*
resolver	*to resolve*
saber	*to know how to*
sentir	*to regret, to feel, to be sorry*
soler (defective)	*to be in the habit of*
sospechar	*to suspect*
temer	*to fear*
tocarle a uno	*to be one's turn*
ver	*to see*

43.4 Los verbos usados con a (Verbs used with a)

Many verbs take the preposition **a** before a following infinitive.

Juana **aprendió a bailar** anoche. *Juana learned to dance last night.*

acercarse a	*to approach, to come near*
acostumbrarse a	*to get accustomed to*
acudir a	*to come to, to resort to*
aficionarse a	*to grow fond of*
alborotarse a	*to get excited about*
animar a	*to encourage to*
aplicarse a	*to apply oneself to*
aprender a	*to learn to*
aprestarse a	*to prepare oneself to*
apresurarse a	*to hurry to*
aspirar a	*to aspire to*
arriesgarse a	*to risk*
atreverse a	*to dare to*
autorizar a	*to authorize to*
ayudar a	*to help to*

bajar a	*to go down to*
comenzar a	*to begin to, to commence to*
contribuir a	*to contribute to*
cooperar a	*to cooperate in*
decidirse a	*to decide to*
dedicarse a	*to dedicate oneself to*
detenerse a	*to stop to*
disponerse a	*to get ready to*
echarse a	*to begin to*
empezar a	*to begin to*
enseñar a	*to teach to*
habituarse a	*to get accustomed to*
invitar a	*to invite to*
ir a	*to go to*
limitarse a	*to limit oneself to*
llegar a	*to arrive at, to become, to succeed in*
llevar a	*to lead to*
negarse a	*to refuse to*
obligar a	*to oblige to, to force to*
ofrecerse a	*to offer to*
oponerse a	*to oppose*
pasar a	*to go on to*
ponerse a	*to begin to*
principiar a	*to begin to*
proponerse a	*to plan to*
referirse a	*to refer to*
renunciar a	*to renounce*
resignarse a	*to resign oneself to*
salir a	*to go out to, to come out to*
subir a	*to climb to*
tender a	*to tend to*
venir a	*to come to*
volver a	*to do again, to return to*

43.5 Los verbos usados con **de** (Verbs used with **de**)

Many verbs take the preposition **de** before a following infinitive.

Me canso de trabajar tanto.   *I'm tired of working so much.*

abstenerse de	*to abstain from*
acabar de	*to have just* + past participle
acordarse de	*to remember to*

aburrirse de	*to be bored*
admirarse de	*to be surprised at*
alegrarse de	*to be glad to*
avisar de	*to warn to*
beneficiarse de	*to benefit from*
cansarse de	*to become tired of*
cesar de	*to stop*
culpar de	*to blame for*
deber de	*must, should*
dejar de	*to stop, to cease*
descuidarse de	*to neglect to*
desistir de	*to give up, to desist from*
disfrutar de	*to enjoy*
dispensar de	*to exempt from*
encargarse de	*to take it upon oneself to*
excusarse de	*to decline to, to excuse oneself for*
felicitar de	*to congratulate on*
gozar de	*to enjoy*
guardarse de	*to take care not to*
haber de	*to have to*
hartarse de	*to gorge oneself, to get fed up with*
informarse de	*to inquire into*
jurar de	*to swear to*
lamentarse de	*to complain of*
notificar de	*to notify to*
ocuparse de	*to take care of*
olvidarse de	*to forget to*
perdonar de	*to pardon for*
persuadir de	*to persuade to*
privarse de	*to deprive oneself of*
regocijarse de	*to rejoice at*
reírse de	*to laugh about*
sufrir de	*to suffer from*
sonreírse de	*to smile about*
tener el antojo de	*to have a craving to*
tener el deber de	*to have the duty to*
tener el derecho de	*to have the right to*
tener el gusto de	*to have the pleasure to*
tener el permiso de	*to have the permission to*
tener el placer de	*to have the pleasure to*
tener el valor de	*to have the courage to*
tener flojera de	*to be lazy about, to feel lazy about*

tener ganas de	*to want to, to have a mind to, to feel like*
tener la audacidad de	*to have the audacity to*
tener la impresión de	*to have the feeling to*
tener la intuición de	*to have the intuition to*
tener la satisfacción de	*to have the satisfaction to*
tener la seguridad de	*to be sure to, to be certain of*
tener miedo de	*to be afraid to*
tener necesidad de	*to have the need to*
tener tiempo de	*to have the time to*
tratar de	*to try to*
tratarse de	*to concern, to be a question of*

43.6 Los verbos usados con con, por, para, en

Many verbs are used with other prepositions before a following infinitive.

amenazar con	*to threaten to*
conformarse con	*to be satisfied to*
contar con	*to expect to, to count on*
contentarse con	*to be satisfied to*
preocuparse con	*to be concerned about*
soñar con	*to dream of*
acabar por	*to finish by, to end up by*
comenzar por	*to start by, to begin by*
empezar por	*to start by, to begin by*
estar por (hacer)	*to remain to (be done)*
esforzarse por	*to strive for, to make an effort to*
interesarse por	*to become interested in*
morirse por	*to be dying to*
preocuparse por	*to worry about, to be concerned with*
esperar para	*to wait to*
estar listo para	*to be ready to*
estar para	*to be about to*
prepararse para	*to prepare oneself to, to get ready to*
trabajar para	*to work to*
consistir en	*to consist of*
consentir en	*to consent to, to agree to*
convenir en	*to agree to, to agree upon*

ejercitarse en	*to practice*
empeñarse en	*to persist in*
esforzarse en	*to strive for, to make an effort to*
insistir en	*to insist on*
obstinarse en	*to persist in*
ocuparse en	*to be engaged in, to be busy with*
pensar en	*to think of, to think about*
perseverar en	*to persevere in, to persist in*
persistir en	*to persist in*
quedar en	*to agree to*
tardar en	*to be long in, to delay in*
vacilar en	*to hesitate to*

43.7 Los verbos y los nombres (Verbs and nouns)

Some verbs are used with a preposition before a noun in Spanish, while the equivalent English verbs are used without a preposition. (See also *La preposición personal* a *19*.)

Me casé con una linda mujer.	*I married a beautiful woman.*

acercarse a	*to approach*
acordarse de	*to remember*
asistir a	*to attend*
casarse con	*to marry*
dar a	*to face*
darse cuenta de	*to realize*
entrar en	*to enter*
fijarse en	*to notice*
jugar a	*to play (a sport)*
partir de	*to leave*
pasar de	*to exceed*
renunciar a	*to renounce*
salir de	*to leave*
servir de	*to act as, to serve as*
servirse de	*to serve oneself, to help oneself*
unirse a	*to join*

43.8 Los verbos usados sin una preposición (Verbs used without a preposition)

A few common verbs in Spanish are not used with a preposition before a noun, although their English equivalents are.

Busqué mis libros por todas partes.
I looked for my books everywhere

buscar	*to look for*
desear	*to wish for*
escuchar	*to listen to*
esperar	*to hope for, to wait for*
mirar	*to look at*
pedir	*to ask for*

44 Los verbos reflexivos

44.1 La formación (Formation)

In Spanish, most verbs taking a direct or indirect object can be used as reflexive verbs with the addition of a reflexive pronoun.

yo	**me lavo**	y	**me visto**
tú	**te lavas**	y	**te vistes**
él, ella, usted	**se lava**	y	**se viste**
nosotros	**nos lavamos**	y	**nos vestimos**
vosotros	**os laváis**	y	**os vestís**
ellos, ellas, ustedes	**se lavan**	y	**se visten**

44.2 La posición de los pronombres reflexivos (Position of reflexive pronouns)

A. Reflexive pronouns normally precede the conjugated verb.

Me levanto a las ocho.   **Nos** escribimos a menudo.
María **se** ausentará un año.   **Te** quejaste sin razón.

B. Reflexive pronouns follow and are attached to affirmative commands.

Siéntate.	Ponte el abrigo.	Levántense.	Váyanse.
Sentaos.[1]	Vestíos.[1]	Vámonos.[2]	Sentémonos.

With negative commands, reflexive pronouns precede the conjugated verb. (See *Placement of personal pronouns 18.1G*.)

---

1. In forming the plural imperative of reflexive verbs, the final **-d** is dropped before the reflexive pronoun **os**. (Exception: irse, **idos**).
2. When the reflexive pronoun **nos** is added to the command form, the final **-s** is dropped from the verb.

C.   Reflexive pronouns follow and are generally attached to infinitives, although they may also precede the conjugated verb.

Voy a lavarme la cara.[3]   or   **Me** voy a lavar la cara.
I am going to wash my face.   *I am going to wash my face.*

D.   Reflexive pronouns are attached to the present participle. In the progressive forms, they may be attached to the present participle or precede the verb **estar.** (See also *Placement of personal pronouns 18.1G.*)

Están desayunándose.   or   **Se** están desayunando.

44.3 El uso (Use)

A.   In a reflexive construction, the subject performs an action upon itself.

Esta mañana **me bañé** temprano.
I took a bath early this morning.

Queremos comprar**nos** un coche nuevo.
We want to buy ourselves a new car.

Se cortó afeitándose.
He cut himself shaving.

Mi amigo **se** puso el sombrero[3] antes de salir.
My friend put on his hat before he went out.

B.   The reciprocal reflexive

A reflexive construction is also used to express an action that two or more agents perform upon each other.

Se escriben cuando están de vacaciones.
They write to each other when they are on vacation.

Ellos **se** conocen desde hace mucho tiempo.
They know each other for a long time.

Nos queremos mucho, por eso **nos** entendemos bien.
We love each other very much, that's why we get along well.

---

3. The definite article and not the possessive adjective is used with parts of the body and articles of clothing in reflexive constructions.

C.   The idiomatic reflexive

Some verbs, when used in their reflexive form, have a different meaning. (See *Most common idiomatic reflexive verbs 44.5.*)

divertir	*to amuse*	**divertirse**	*to have fun*
acostar	*to lay down*	**acostarse**	*to go to bed*
dormir	*to sleep*	**dormirse**	*to fall asleep*

D.   The essentially reflexive

Certain verbs are used only in a reflexive form. (See *Essentially reflexive verbs 44.4.*)

suicidarse	*to commit suicide*
arrepentirse de	*to regret, to repent*
quejarse de	*to complain about*

E.   A reflexive construction may be used to convey the idea of an action performed by an indefinite subject. The pronoun **se** is then used with the third person singular of the verb.

No **se puede** fumar en clase.
Smoking is not permitted in class.

Se bebe mucho vino en Francia.
They drink a lot of wine in France.

Se dice que el presidente está enfermo.
They say that the President is sick.

Se come bien en este restaurante.
One eats well in this restaurant.

If this construction is used with a verb which is already reflexive, the impersonal subject **uno** is added.

Uno se defiende como puede.
One defends oneself anyway one can.

F.   The reflexive is used to substitute for the passive voice when the agent is not expressed. The verb is in the third person singular or plural depending upon the subject.

Se escribieron muchas novelas sobre este tema.
Many novels were written on this subject.

Se venden muchas cosas en esta tienda.
Many things are sold in this store.

Aquí se habla francés.
French is spoken here.

Se compra oro.
We buy gold (gold is bought).

44.4 Essentially reflexive verbs

aborrascarse	*to become stormy*
abotagarse	*to become swollen, puffy*
abstenerse	*to abstain, to refrain*
acalenturarse	*to become feverish*
acatarrarse	*to catch a cold*
acuclillarse	*to squat*
acurrucarse	*to curl up, to huddle*
adormilarse	*to doze*
adueñarse	*to take possession*
agusanarse	*to become worm-ridden*
amancebarse	*to live in concubinage*
amodorrarse	*to become drowsy*
antojarse	*to fancy, to feel like, to have a notion to*
apoltronarse	*to become lazy, idle*
arranciarse	*to become rancid*
arrellanarse	*to make oneself comfortable*
arrepentirse	*to regret, to repent*
atragantarse	*to choke*
atreverse	*to dare*
ausentarse	*to absent oneself*
bifurcarse	*to bifurcate, to branch off*
compenetrarse	*to compenetrate, to get fully acquainted*
conexionarse	*to make social or commercial connections*
contorcerse	*to writhe, to distort one's features*
desayunarse	*to have breakfast*

desentenderse	*to feign ignorance*
desgañitarse	*to scream at the top of one's voice*
despreocuparse	*to put aside one's cares, to neglect*
desvivirse	*to be eager, to be anxious to please*
emberrincharse	*to fly into a tantrum*
emperrarse	*to be stubborn*
enamoricarse	*to become infatuated with*
encabritarse	*to lurch upward*
encorajinarse	*to get angry*
endeudarse	*to go into debt*
endrogarse	*to take drugs, to go into debt (Mex.)*
enfrascarse	*to become entangled or involved*
enfurruñarse	*to get angry, peeved*
escabullirse	*to sneak away, to slip through*
espatarrarse	*to fall with one's legs wide apart*
expatriarse	*to go into exile*
extasiarse	*to become ecstatic*
fosilizarse	*to fossilize*
gangrenarse	*to become gangrenous*
grietarse	*to crack, to split*
guillarse	*to flee, to lose one's head*
hipertrofiarse	*to become hypertrophied*
incautarse	*to seize money or property*
indisciplinarse	*to become undisciplined, unruly*
inveterarse	*to become firmly established; to become old*
jactarse	*to boast, to brag*
macarse	*to begin to rot, to spoil*
masturbarse	*to masturbate*
mirlarse	*to put on airs*
obstinarse	*to persist, to be stubborn*
osificarse	*to ossify*
personarse	*to have an interview, to appear in person*
pomponearse	*to show off*
precaucionarse	*to take precautions*
prosternarse	*to prostrate oneself*
querellarse	*to file a complaint, to lament*
ramificarse	*to ramify, to branch off*
rebelarse	*to revolt, to rebel*
remilgarse	*to behave in an affected manner*

repantigarse	*to sprawl out*
repapilarse	*to glut*
resentirse	*to become resentful, to feel hurt*
retreparse	*to lean back in a chair*
revotarse	*to reverse one's vote*
ruborizarse	*to blush*
sobreverterse	*to run over, to overflow*
sucintarse	*to be succinct*
suicidarse	*to commit suicide*
transparentarse	*to show through*
trastrabarse	*to stammer, to become tongue-tied*
trazumarse	*to ooze, to seep, to exude*
unfanarse	*to pride oneself, to boast*
volquearse	*to roll about, to roll over*

44.5 Most common idiomatic reflexive verbs

acostarse	*to go to bed*	**acostar**	*to lay down*
apoderarse de	*to appropriate*	**apoderar**	*to empower*
burlarse de	*to make fun of*	**burlar**	*to outwit, to deceive*
darse cuenta de	*to realize*	**dar**	*to give*
despedirse de	*to say good-bye*	**despedir**	*to discharge, to emit*
dirigirse a	*to go to, to address*	**dirigir**	*to direct*
distinguirse	*to excel*	**distinguir**	*to distinguish*
dormirse	*to fall asleep*	**dormir**	*to sleep*
encontrarse con	*to meet*	**encontrar**	*to find*
entenderse con	*to get along*	**entender**	*to understand*
enterarse de	*to find out*	**enterar**	*to inform*
entregarse	*to surrender*	**entregar**	*to deliver*
establecerse	*to get settled*	**establecer**	*to establish*
hacerse	*to become, to pretend*	**hacer**	*to make, to do*
hallarse	*to be present*	**hallar**	*to find, to discover*
irse	*to leave*	**ir**	*to go*
llamarse	*to be called*	**llamar**	*to call*
llevarse	*to carry off, to get along*	**llevar**	*to take, to carry*
marcharse	*to leave*	**marchar**	*to walk*
negarse	*to refuse*	**negar**	*to deny*
ocuparse de	*to attend to*	**ocupar**	*to occupy*

ponerse	*to put on, to become*	**poner**	*to put*
ponerse a	*to begin*		
pasarse de	*to exceed*	**pasar**	*to pass*
presentarse	*to appear*	**presentar**	*to introduce, to present*
reunirse	*to meet, to gather*	**reunir**	*to collect*
sentirse (mal)	*to feel (ill)*	**sentir**	*to regret, to feel*
tratarse de	*to be a question of*	**tratar de**	*to try to*
volverse	*to become, to turn*	**volver**	*to return*

45 El estilo indirecto

A. Indirect discourse is used to relate a statement or a dialog without quoting the exact words.

   1. To relate a sentence expressing a statement or a fact, **que** + conjugated verb are used.

   Roberto: —Estoy contento de mi trabajo.
   Roberto **dice que está** contento de su trabajo.

   2. To relate an interrogative thought as a statement and not a question, **si** + conjugated verb are used.

   Roberto: —¿Escribes a tu madre?
   Roberto **me pregunta si escribo** a mi madre.

   Roberto: —¿Es un buen libro?
   Roberto **me pregunta si es** un buen libro.

   Interrogative words are repeated in indirect discourse.

   —¿**Cuánto** dinero tiene usted?
   Él me pregunta **cuánto** dinero tengo.

   —¿**Cuál** es su profesión?
   Él quiere saber **cuál** es mi profesión.

   —¿**Por qué** salen tan temprano?
   Nos pregunta **por qué** salimos tan temprano.

   The interrogative word **qué** is often replaced by the expression **lo que**.

   —¿**Qué** está haciendo?
   Me pregunta **lo que** estoy haciendo. *or*
   Me pregunta **qué** estoy haciendo.

3. To relate a sentence expressing a command or an order, the imperative form is replaced by **que** + present subjunctive.

El profesor: – ¡Hablen despacio!
El profesor **nos pide que hablemos** despacio.

Mi madre me dice: – ¡Cierra la puerta!
Mi madre **me dice que cierre** la puerta.

The expression **dar la orden de** + infinitive may be used in place of the subjunctive mood.

Mi madre **me da la orden de cerrar** la puerta.

B. Sequence of tenses

1. The present tense in direct discourse is replaced by the imperfect in indirect discourse when the introductory verb is in the past tense.

—Sus composiciones son excelentes.
Él **dijo** que mis composiciones **eran** excelentes.

Él dijo shows that you are relating a past action; **son** therefore, becomes **eran**. Following the same pattern:

VERB IN DIRECT DISCOURSE		VERB IN INDIRECT DISCOURSE
Present	becomes	Imperfect
Preterit Present perfect }	become	Pluperfect
Future	becomes	Conditional
Future perfect	becomes	Conditional perfect
Imperative Present subjunctive }	become	Imperfect subjunctive

The other tenses do not change.

Luis: —**Creo** que Alicia **tiene** razón. (*present*)
Luis **dijo que creía** que Alicia **tenía** razón. (*imperfect*)

Luis: —**Vi** a mi hermana ayer. (*preterit*)
Luis: —**He visto** a mi hermana ayer. (*present perfect*)
Luis **dijo que había visto** a su hermana el día anterior. (*pluperfect*)

Luis: —**Iré** a ver a mi madre. (*future*)
Luis **dijo que iría** a ver a su madre. (*conditional*)
Luis: —Para entonces **habré terminado** mi trabajo. (*future perfect*)
Luis **contestó que** para entonces **habría terminado** su trabajo. (*conditional perfect*)
Luis: —**Llama** a Alicia por teléfono. (*imperative*)
Luis: —**Quiero que llames** a Alicia por teléfono. (*present subjunctive*)
Luis **me sugirió que llamara** a Alicia por teléfono. (*imperfect subjunctive*)

2. The sequence of tenses applies to any compound sentence in Spanish. The verb in the dependent clause conveying a chronological relationship must be changed if the verb in the main clause is changed to a past tense.

Pienso que Jorge **tiene** ganas de comprar un coche. (*present*)
Pensé que Jorge **tenía** ganas de comprar un coche. (*imperfect*)

Ella **me dice que olvidó** sus llaves. (*preterit*)
Ella **me dijo que había olvidado** sus llaves. (*pluperfect*)

Estamos seguros que pasarán buenas vacaciones. (*future*)
Estábamos seguros que pasarían buenas vacaciones. (*conditional*)

C. Changes in adjectives, pronouns, and time expressions in indirect discourse

1. Adjectives and pronouns

Luis: —**Te** presto **mi** coche.
Luis **me** dijo que me prestaría **su** coche.

2. Expressions of time and place

hoy	becomes	**aquel día**
mañana	becomes	**el día siguiente**
pasado mañana	becomes	**a los dos días**
ayer	becomes	**la víspera**
anoche	becomes	**la noche anterior**
anteayer	becomes	**la antevíspera**
antenoche	becomes	**dos noches antes**
aquí	becomes	**allí**
el lunes próximo	becomes	**el lunes siguiente**
el mes próximo	becomes	**el mes siguiente**
ahora	becomes	**en aquel momento**

To other expressions of time, add **aquel** or **aquella**: **aquel verano,
aquella mañana, aquella tarde,** and so on.

D.   Common verbs to express indirect discourse

aconsejar	**contestar**	**objetar**
admitir	**decir**	**ordenar**
advertir	**declarar**	**pedir**
afirmar	**disponer**	**preguntar**
agregar	**explicar**	**recomendar**
anunciar	**gritar**	**reconocer**
añadir	**indicar**	**repetir**
asegurar	**insinuar**	**responder**
comprobar	**mandar**	**sugerir**

46 La voz pasiva

A. The passive voice is formed with **ser** and the past participle of a verb that takes a direct object. The past participle agrees in number and gender with the subject. Any tense may be used.

B. Active voice

El profesor (*subject*) **corrige** (*active voice*) **las composiciones** (*direct object*).

Passive voice

Las composiciones (*subject*) **son corregidas** (*passive voice*) **por el profesor** (*agent*).

Las composiciones fueron corregidas por el profesor.
Las composiciones eran corregidas por el profesor.
Las composiciones han sido corregidas por el profesor.
Las composiciones habían sido corregidas por el profesor.
Las composiciones serán corregidas por el profesor.
Las composiciones habrán sido corregidas por el profesor.
Es necesario que las composiciones sean corregidas por el profesor.
Dudo que las composiciones hayan sido corregidas por el profesor.

C. The direct object in the active sentence becomes the subject in the passive, while the subject becomes the agent, usually introduced by the preposition **por**. The agent may be preceded by the preposition **de** with verbs denoting emotion, such as **amar, querer,** and **odiar,** or with verbs such as **saber** and **conocer.**

Alicia y Pablo **son queridos de todos.**
Es sabido de todos que más vale prevenir que curar.

When the subject in the active voice is indefinite, no agent is expressed in the passive voice.

Robaron mi coche anoche.
Se robó mi coche anoche.
Mi coche fue robado anoche.

D.   A reflexive construction is often used in place of the passive voice when the
     agent is not stated. (See also *Los verbos reflexivos 44.3E.*)

Se hacen muchos errores.	*Many mistakes are made.*
Se habla francés.	*French is spoken.*
Se robó mi coche anoche.	*My car was stolen last night.*
Se alquilan habitaciones.	*Rooms for rent (rooms are rented).*

47 El presente de subjuntivo

47.1 La formación (Formation)

A. The present subjunctive is formed by dropping the -o ending of the first person singular of the present indicative and adding the present subjunctive endings.

	amar	comer	vivir
	am~~o~~	com~~o~~	viv~~o~~
que yo	ame	coma	viva
que tú	ames	comas	vivas
que él, ella, usted	ame	coma	viva
que nosotros	amemos	comamos	vivamos
que vosotros	améis	comáis	viváis
que ellos, ellas, ustedes	amen	coman	vivan

B. The stem of the present subjunctive of most irregular verbs is formed the same way.

caber	yo quep~~o~~	que yo **quepa**, que tú **quepas**, etc.
caer	yo caig~~o~~	que yo **caiga**, que tú **caigas**, etc.
decir	yo dig~~o~~	que yo **diga**, que tú **digas**, etc.
hacer	yo hag~~o~~	que yo **haga**, que tú **hagas**, etc.
oír	yo oig~~o~~	que yo **oiga**, que tú **oigas**, etc.
poder	yo pued~~o~~	que yo **pueda**, que tú **puedas**[1]
poner	yo pong~~o~~	que yo **ponga**, que tú **pongas**, etc.
querer	yo quier~~o~~	que yo **quiera**, que tú **quieras**[2]
salir	yo salg~~o~~	que yo **salga**, que tú **salgas**, etc.

---

1. The plural forms are: **podamos, podáis, puedan**
2. The plural forms are: **queramos, queráis, quieran**

tener	yo teng∅	que yo **tenga**, que tú **tengas**, etc.
traer	yo traig∅	que yo **traiga**, que tú **traigas**, etc.
valer	yo valg∅	que yo **valga**, que tú **valgas**, etc.
venir	yo veng∅	que yo **venga**, que tú **vengas**, etc.
ver	yo ve∅	que yo **vea**, que tú **veas**, etc.

C.   Completely irregular in the present subjunctive are:

	dar	**ir**	**ser**
que yo	**dé**	**vaya**	**sea**
que tú	**des**	**vayas**	**seas**
que él, ella, usted	**dé**	**vaya**	**sea**
que nosotros	**demos**	**vayamos**	**seamos**
que vosotros	**deis**	**vayáis**	**seáis**
que ellos, ellas, ustedes	**den**	**vayan**	**sean**

	haber	**estar**	**saber**
que yo	**haya**	**esté**	**sepa**
que tú	**hayas**	**estés**	**sepas**
que él, ella, usted	**haya**	**esté**	**sepa**
que nosotros	**hayamos**	**estemos**	**sepamos**
que vosotros	**hayáis**	**estéis**	**sepáis**
que ellos, ellas, ustedes	**hayan**	**estén**	**sepan**

D.   Some regular verbs have orthographical changes in the present subjunctive. (See *Los verbos regulares con cambios ortográficos 29.*)

buscar	que yo **busque**, etc.
llegar	que yo **llegue**, etc.
gozar	que yo **goce**, etc.
averiguar	que yo **averigüe**, etc.
recoger	que yo **recoja**, etc.
exigir	que yo **exija**, etc.
ejercer	que yo **ejerza**, etc.
fruncir	que yo **frunza**, etc.
distinguir	que yo **distinga**, etc.
delinquir	que yo **delinca**, etc.

47.2 El uso (Use)

The indicative mood presents an action or a state as a fact. The subjunctive, however, is the mood of possibility. It is used almost exclusively in dependent clauses introduced by **que**, which is always included. The use of a subjunctive in a dependent clause depends upon the idea expressed in the main clause.

The present subjunctive is used when the following two conditions are met in a sentence: (1) the action expressed by the dependent verb is simultaneous with or future to the action of the main verb, and (2) the verb in the main clause expresses:

A.   Doubt or uncertainty.

Dudamos que vengan esta noche.
We doubt they'll come tonight.

Pablo **no está seguro que vengan** sus padres.
Pablo is not sure his parents will come.

B.   Negation.

Niego que Marta lo **tenga.**
I deny that Marta has it.

No es cierto que mi tía **esté** aquí.
It isn't true that my aunt is here.

C.   Desire, prohibition, or indirect commands.

Quiero que salgan inmediatamente.
I want you (them) to leave immediately.

Su familia **quiere que vaya** a la universidad.
His (her) family wants him (her) to go to the university.

Prohiben que yo **fume.**
They forbid me to smoke.

Les digo que se levanten.
I'm telling you to get up.

El profesor **exije que estemos** a tiempo.
The professor requires us to be on time.

D.   Necessity.

Es preciso que ellos **vengan**.
It is essential that they come.

Es necesario que se pongan a estudiar.
It is necessary that they begin to study.

E.   Permission, approval, or disapproval.

Consiento que lo **hagan**.
I agree that you (they) do it.

Apruebo que le **escriban**.
I approve that you (they) write to him (her, you).

Dejan que fumen.
They allow them to smoke.

F.   An emotional feeling (joy, sorrow, fear, and so on).

Celebramos que apruebes el curso.
We are happy that you are passing the course.

Temo que haga mucho frío este invierno.
I'm afraid that it will be very cold this winter.

Siento que no **puedan** venir con nosotros.
I am sorry they can't come with us.

Espero que no se lo **olviden**.
I hope you (they) won't forget it.

Lamentamos que no **vengan**.
We are sorry they are not coming.

47.3 The subjunctive is used

A.   When the antecedent of a relative pronoun is uncertain or nonexistent.

Busco **un hotel que** no **esté** muy lejos.
I am looking for a hotel not too far away.

No tiene **ningún amigo que** le **sea** fiel.
He (she) hasn't a faithful friend.

No hay **mujer que sea** perfecta.
There is no perfect woman.

¿Conoce usted a **alguien que pueda** ayudarme?
Do you know anybody who could help me?

B. When the antecedent is a superlative and after the expressions:

el único (los únicos, la única, las únicas)
el primero (los primeros, la primera, las primeras)
el último (los últimos, la última, las últimas)

Es **el único** medicamento **que pueda** ayudarle.
It's the only medication that can help him.

París es **la ciudad más bonita que** yo **conozca.**
Paris is the most beautiful city I know.

C. After certain conjunctions.

sin que	*without*
salvo que	*unless*
a menos que	*unless*
a no ser que	*unless*
por temor (de) que	*for fear that*
por miedo (de) que	*for fear that*
con tal (de) que	*provided that*
a condición (de) que	*provided that*
siempre que	*provided that*
antes (de) que	*before, sooner than*
en caso (de) que	*in case (that)*
según que	*according to whether*
como si	*as if*
a fin de que	*in order that, so that*
con objeto de que	*in order that, so that*
para que	*in order that, so that*
suponiendo que	*supposing that*

Antes que salgas, apaga la luz.
Before you leave, turn off the light.

Él trabaja **para que** usted **descanse.**
He works so that you may rest.

Dale una pluma a Luis **para que firme** la solicitud.
Give a pen to Luis so he can sign the application.

Te acompañaré **con tal que consiga** el dinero.
I will accompany you provided that I get the money.

Haré la cama **en caso de que venga.**
I'll make the bed in case he (she, you) will come.

D.   After the following conjunctions, only when future time is implied. The
       indicative is used when the clause expresses present or past time.

hasta que	*until*
luego que	*as soon as*
en cuanto	*as soon as*
tan pronto como	*as soon as*
cuando	*when*
después (de) que	*after*
mientras (que)	*while, as long as*

Se lo **diré cuando venga.**
I'll tell him when he comes.

But:

Se lo **dije cuando vino.**
I told him when he came.

Me acostaré **después de que salgan** ustedes.
I'll go to bed after you leave.

But:

Me acosté **después de que salieron** ustedes.
I went to bed after you left.

E.   After **quizá, quizás, tal vez,** and **acaso** (maybe), when future time is
       implied. The subjunctive or the indicative may be used when the past or
       the present is implied.

Quizá(s) vengan hoy. (*future*)   **Tal vez apruebe** el examen. (*future*)
Quizá(s) vinieron ayer. (*past*)   **Tal vez aprobaron** el examen. (*past*)
Quizá(s) hayan venido. (*past*)   **Tal vez hayan aprobado** el examen. (*past*)

F.   With some conjunctions, the speaker determines whether he is going to use the subjunctive or the indicative, depending upon the idea he wishes to convey. The subjunctive is used to express a mere possibility. The indicative is used to express a fact.

aunque	*although, even though*	**no obstante**	*in spite of*
a pesar de que	*in spite of*	**aun cuando**	*even when*

Saldremos **aunque llueva.**
We'll go out even though it may rain.

Saldremos **aunque llueve.**
We'll go out even though it is raining.

G.   After the conjunctions **de manera que** and **de modo que,** the indicative is used when a result is expressed and the subjunctive is used when purpose is expressed.

El profesor habló **de manera que le entendimos.**
The professor spoke in such a way that we understood him.

El profesor habla **de manera que le entendamos.**
The professor speaks so that we may understand him.

H.   After the expression **por . . . que.**

Por más que haga, nunca llegaré.
No matter how much I do, I'll never get there.

Por más inteligente que sea, no aprobará su examen sin estudiar.
No matter how intelligent he is, he won't pass his exam without studying.

Por mucho dinero que tenga, no lo aprovecha.
However much money he has, he doesn't make good use of it.

I.   In clauses introduced by the following indefinite pronouns.

quienquiera, quienesquiera	*whoever, anyone, anybody*
cualquier, cualquiera	*whatever*
cualesquier, cualesquiera	*whatever*
cuandoquiera	*whenever*
comoquiera	*however*
dondequiera	*wherever*

Te lo mandaré **dondequiera que esté**.
Me gusta ir de viaje **comoquiera que sea**.
Dondequiera que él **vaya**, yo voy.

J. After impersonal expressions that express necessity, doubt, emotion, feeling, and so on. (See *Las expresiones impersonales y el subjuntivo 52.*)

Es necesario que mi hijo **estudie**.
It is essential that my son study.

Es lástima que no vengan a la fiesta.
It's a pity they (you) are not coming to the party.

K. In clauses to express a command in the third person singular or plural. In such cases, the main verb requiring the subjunctive is supressed.

¡(Quiero) Que **salgan** inmediatamente!
Let them leave immediately!

¡Que lo **haga** Luis!
Let Luis do it!

¡Que Dios os **bendiga**!
God bless you!

L. After the expressions **ojalá** and **Dios quiera**.

¡Ojalá no llueva!
I hope it will not rain!

¡Ojalá que vengan!
I hope they will come!

¡Dios quiera que esté en casa!
I hope he is home!

M. In certain idiomatic expressions.

¡**Así** sea!   *So be it!*
¡**Viva México**!   *Hurrah for Mexico!*

47.4 The subjunctive is not used

A. When the verb or expression in the main clause expresses a certainty. The indicative is then used for all tenses.

Estoy seguro que vendrán.
El profesor **dice que hago** muchas equivocaciones.
Ella **sabe que** la **llamé** por teléfono.
Es evidente que los periódicos no **dicen** todo.

B. After the verbs **pensar** and **creer** in affirmative sentences. These verbs
    are generally followed by the subjunctive in a negative or interrogative
    sentence, however, because of the implication of doubt.

Pienso que su hermano **está** enfermo.
No pienso que su hermano **esté** enfermo.
Creo que vendrán.
¿Cree usted **que vengan?**

C. When the subject of the main verb and the dependent verb is the same.
    The infinitive is then used.

Mi padre prefiere saber la verdad.
Mi padre prefiere que yo sepa la verdad.

No me gusta llegar tarde.
No me gusta que usted llegue tarde.

Quiero estudiar la lección.
Quiero que estudies la lección.

Me acosté después de comer.
Me acosté después de que salieron ustedes.

D. After impersonal expressions, when a subject is not expressed or
    implied. The infinitive is then used.

Es impossible hacerlo.
Es necesario comer para vivir.

E. After certain verbs such as **mandar, dejar, permitir**, and **aconsejar**, the
    infinitive or the subjunctive may be used. With these verbs, the subject
    of the dependent verb is expressed as the object of the main verb.

Mi madre **nos dejará dormir** tarde.
Mi madre **nos dejará que durmamos** tarde.

Me manda esperar.
Me manda que espere.

Te aconsejo ir.
Te aconsejo que vayas.

48 El imperfecto de subjuntivo

48.1 La formación (Formation)

To form the imperfect subjunctive of all verbs, drop -**ron** from the third person plural of the preterit indicative and add the endings -**ra**, -**ras**, -**ra**, -́**ramos**, -**rais**, -**ran**, or -**se**, -**ses**, -**se**, -́**semos**, -**seis**, -**sen**. The two forms of the imperfect subjunctive are interchangeable.

	amar	comer	vivir
	amar̸o̸n̸	comier̸o̸n̸	vivier̸o̸n̸
que yo	amara	comiera	viviera
que tú	amaras	comieras	vivieras
que él, ella, usted	amara	comiera	viviera
que nosotros	amáramos	comiéramos	viviéramos
que vosotros	amarais	comierais	vivierais
que ellos, ellas, ustedes	amaran	comieran	vivieran
	amar̸o̸n̸	comier̸o̸n̸	vivier̸o̸n̸
que yo	amase	comiese	viviese
que tú	amases	comieses	vivieses
que él, ella, usted	amase	comiese	viviese
que nosotros	amásemos	comiésemos	viviésemos
que vosotros	amaseis	comieseis	vivieseis
que ellos, ellas, ustedes	amasen	comiesen	viviesen

Stem-changing and irregular verbs follow the same procedure.

caber	cupieron	**cupiera**	or	**cupiese**
decir	dijeron	**dijera**	or	**dijese**
estar	estuvieron	**estuviera**	or	**estuviese**
haber	hubieron	**hubiera**	or	**hubiese**
conducir	condujeron	**condujera**	or	**condujese**

| leer | leyeron | **leyera** | or | **leyese** |
| dormir | durmieron | **durmiera** | or | **durmiese** |

48.2 El uso (Use)

A.   The imperfect subjunctive is used when the subjunctive mood is required and when the verb in the main clause is in a past tense or in the conditional.

El profesor $\left\{\begin{array}{l}\textbf{mandó}\\\textbf{mandaba}\\\textbf{mandaría}\\\textbf{había mandado}\\\textbf{habría mandado}\\\textbf{hubiera mandado}\end{array}\right\}$ **que yo hablara (hablase).**

B.   The imperfect subjunctive is used when the action of the dependent verb is already completed at the time expressed by the main verb.

Dudo que Juan **llamara.**   *I doubt that Juan called.*

C.   A more polite form of **querer, poder,** or **deber** is rendered by the **-ra** form of the imperfect subjunctive.

Quisiera ir con usted.
I would like to go with you.

¿Pudiera usted esperar un momento?
Could you wait a moment?

Debiéramos ayudar a aquel señor.
We should help that gentleman.

D.   The imperfect subjunctive is used in an *if*-clause when the conditional is used in the result clause.[1] (See *Las cláusulas condicionales 40.*)

Si **fuéramos** ricos, estaríamos siempre de viaje.
If we were rich, we would always be traveling.

Llegarían a tiempo si **tomaran (tomasen)** el avión.
They would arrive on time if they took the plane.

The **-ra** form of the imperfect subjunctive may also be used in the result clause.

---

1.   When **si** means whether, the indicative is used.
     No sé **si vendrán** esta noche. Me preguntaron **si** había ido.

Si **fuéramos** ricos, **estuviéramos** siempre de viaje.

E.   After the expression **como si**, the imperfect subjunctive or the pluperfect subjunctive is used. (See also *El pluscuamperfecto de subjuntivo 49.2.*)

Le hablé **como si fuera** su padre.
I talked to him (her, you) as if I were his (her, your) father.

Corre **como si tuviera** diez años.
He (she) runs as if he (she) were ten years old.

49 Los tiempos compuestos del subjuntivo

49.1 El perfecto de subjuntivo (Present perfect subjunctive)

A. Formation

The present perfect subjunctive is formed with the present subjunctive of the auxiliary verb **haber** and a past participle.

haya amado	**haya comido**	**haya vivido**
hayas amado, etc.	**hayas comido**, etc.	**hayas vivido**, etc.

B. Use

The present perfect subjunctive is used in a dependent clause to express an action that has happened or will have happened. The verb in the main clause is generally in the present or future and requires a subjunctive verb.

Siento que no **hayan venido.**
I am sorry you didn't come.

¿Nos **avisará** usted **después que hayan conseguido** ellos los boletos?
Will you notify us after they'll have obtained the tickets?

49.2 El pluscuamperfecto de subjuntivo (Pluperfect subjunctive)

A. Formation

The pluperfect subjunctive is formed with the imperfect subjunctive of the verb **haber** and a past participle.

hubiera (hubiese) amado	**hubiera (hubiese) comido**
hubieras (hubieses) amado, etc.	**hubieras (hubieses) comido**, etc.

B. Use

The pluperfect subjunctive is used in a dependent clause to indicate an action already completed at the time expressed by the main verb. The main verb is in a past tense and requires the subjunctive.

Prefería que tú lo **hubieras hecho** antes.
I would prefer that you had done it before.

Dudé que Juana **hubiera llamado.**
I doubted that Juana had called.

¿Creían ustedes **que** yo **hubiera hecho** tal cosa?
Did you believe that I had done such a thing?

C. After the expression **como si**, the pluperfect subjunctive or the imperfect subjunctive is used. (See also *El imperfecto de subjuntivo 48.2E.*)

Jorge corre **como si tuviera** diez años. (*Imperfect subjunctive*)
Jorge runs as if he were ten years old.

Jorge corría **como si hubiera robado** un banco. (*Pluperfect subjunctive*)
Jorge was running as if he had robbed a bank.

50 La correlación de los tiempos

MAIN CLAUSE		DEPENDENT CLAUSE
imperative	que ⎫	present subjunctive
present indicative	que ⎪	(when past action is not indicated)
future indicative	que ⎬	present perfect subjunctive
present perfect indicative	que ⎭	(when past action is indicated)
imperfect indicative	que ⎫	imperfect subjunctive
preterit indicative	que ⎪	or
pluperfect indicative	que ⎬	pluperfect subjunctive
conditional	que ⎭	

(See also *Las cláusulas condicionales 40.*)

Alégrese
Be happy

Me alegro
I am happy

de que Luis lo **haga.**
that Louis is doing it.

Me alegraré
I'll be happy

de que Luis lo **haya hecho.**
that Louis has done it.

Me he alegrado
I was happy

Me alegraba
I was happy

Me alegré
I became happy

de que Luis lo **hiciera.**
that Louis did it.

Me había alegrado
I had been happy

de que Luis lo **hubiera hecho.**
that Louis had done it.

Me alegraría
I would be happy

51 Los verbos que requieren el subjuntivo

Following are the most common verbs which require the subjunctive in a following dependent clause.

acceder a	empeñar(se)	obligar a
aceptar	entristecer(se)	oponerse a
aconsejar	esperar	ordenar
agradecer	estar alegre	pedir
alegrarse	estar cansado	permitir
anhelar	estar contento	preferir
ansiar	estar encantado	pretender
aprobar	estar enojado	precisar
asustarse	estar feliz	procurar
bastar	estar indignado	prohibir
celebrar	estar orgulloso	propiciar
confiar en	estar satisfecho	proponer
consentir	estar triste	querer
contentar(se)	evitar	rechazar
convenir	exigir	refutar
decidir	extrañar	rogar
decretar	favorecer	sentir
dejar	gustar	sorprenderse
deplorar	impedir	sospechar
desaprobar	importar	sugerir
desear	insistir en	suplicar
disponer	lamentar	suponer
doler	mandar	temer
dudar	necesitar	tener miedo
emocionar(se)	negar	tolerar

52 Las expresiones impersonales y el subjuntivo

A. Following are the most common impersonal expressions which are followed by the subjunctive.

es absurdo que	es inútil que	es urgente que
es aconsejable que	es justo que	es útil que
es agradable que	es lamentable que	no es cierto que
es bueno que	es lástima que	no es claro que
es comprensible que	es malo que	no es evidente que
es conveniente que	es maravilloso que	no es seguro que
es curioso que	es mejor que	no es verdad que
es de temerse que	es natural que	basta que
es delicado que	es necesario que	conviene que
es difícil que	es penoso que	consta que
es discutible que	es peor que	da pena que
es dudoso que	es posible que	da vergüenza que
es esencial que	es preciso que	gusta que
es fácil que	es preferible que	importa que
es falso que	es probable que	molesta que
es hora de que	es raro que	parece imposible que
es importante que	es ridículo que	parece mentira que
es imposible que	es sorprendente que	parece raro que
es improbable que	es suficiente que	puede ser que
es indispensable que	es tiempo de que	se necesita que
es injusto que	es triste que	se puede que
es innegable que	es una suerte que	vale más que

B.   An impersonal expression followed by an infinitive conveys a very general meaning. (See also *47.4D*.)

Es imposible dormir cuando hay mucho ruido.
It is impossible to sleep when there is a lot of noise.

Es necesario trabajar para ganarse la vida.
It is necessary to work in order to earn a living.

53 El verbo hacer

53.1 Hacer + el infinitivo (Hacer + the infinitive)

When followed by an infinitive, **hacer** is causative; that is, the subject of **hacer** causes an action to be done by another person.

Luis **hace lavar** su coche.
Luis has his car washed.

El profesor **los hace estudiar**.
The professor forces them to study.

53.2 Hacer y las expresiones temporales (Hacer in time expressions)

Hace + time expression + **que**, followed by a verb in the present indicative, expresses an action or condition which started in the past and is still continuing.

Hace cinco años que vivo en Los Ángeles.
I have been living in Los Angeles for five years.

¿Cuánto tiempo hace que no los **ves?**
How long is it that you are not seeing them?

Hacía + time expression + **que**, followed by a verb in the imperfect indicative, expresses an action or condition which started in the past and continued until a specific moment in the past.

Hacía dos años que trabajaba allí cuando perdí mi empleo.
I was working there two years when I lost my job.

¿Cuánto tiempo hacía que no los **veías?**
How long was it that you were not seeing them?

When the verbal expression precedes the **hacer** construction, **desde hace** and **desde hacía** are used.

Vivo en Los Ángeles **desde hace cinco años.**
Trabajaba allí **desde hacía dos años** cuando perdí mi empleo.

Hace + time expression following a verb in the preterit or imperfect indicative means *ago*. Note that **que** is not used in this construction.

Recibí mi diploma **hace tres años.**
I got my degree three years ago.

Hace diez años vivía todavía con mis padres.
Ten years ago, I was still living with my parents.

53.3 Los modismos con **hacer** (Idiomatic expressions with **hacer**)

A.   To express weather

Hace buen tiempo.	*The weather is fine.*
Hace mal tiempo.	*The weather is bad.*
Hace calor.	*It is warm.*
Hace frío.	*It is cold.*
Hace fresco.	*It is cool.*
Hace viento.	*It is windy.*
Hace sol.	*It is sunny.*
Hace luna.	*There is a moon.*
Se hace tarde.	*It is getting late.*

But:

Llovizna; está lloviznando.	*It is drizzling.*
Nieva; está nevando.	*It is snowing.*
Llueve; está lloviendo.	*It is raining.*
Truena; está tronando.	*It is thundering.*
Está helando.	*It is freezing.*
Es de día.	*It is daylight.*
Es de noche.	*It is dark.*
Está oscuro.	*It is dark.*
Hay lodo.	*It is muddy.*
Hay brisa.	*There is a breeze.*
Hay humedad.	*It is humid.*

B.   Other idiomatic expressions with **hacer**

hacer alusión	*to allude*

hacer burla de	*to make fun of*
hacer caso	*to mind, to pay attention*
hacer cola	*to stand in line*
hacer conocer	*to make known*
hacer daño	*to hurt*
hacer de	*to act as*
hacer el favor de + inf.	*please* + imperative
hacer el papel de	*to play the part of*
hacer escala	*to stop over (plane or boat)*
hacer falta	*to need, to be lacking, to miss*
hacer gestos	*to gesture, to gesticulate*
hacer hincapié	*to emphasize*
hacer pedazos	*to break or tear to pieces*
hacer señas	*to signal*
hacer un viaje	*to take a trip*
hacer una pregunta	*to ask a question*
hacer una visita	*to pay a visit*
hacerse abogado	*to become a lawyer*
hacerse amigos	*to become friends*
hacerse cargo de	*to take charge of*
hacer(se) el tonto	*to act dumb*

54 Los verbos <u>conocer</u> y <u>saber</u>

54.1 conocer

Conocer means *to know* in the sense of to be acquainted with a person or a thing—a city, a movie, a book, a story, a play, and so on.

No **conozco** la China.
¿**Conoce** usted a mi padre?
Pablo **conoce** muy bien el camino.

54.2 saber

A.   **Saber** means *to know* (intellectually), that is, to possess knowledge. Hence, it can never be used with a person.

¿**Sabe** usted si viene Jorge?
No **sé** la lección.

B.   **Saber** + infinitive means *to know how.*

¿**Sabe** usted hablar japonés?
No **sé** tocar la guitarra.

55 El verbo deber

A. The basic meaning of the verb **deber** is *to owe*.

Debo diez dólares a mi hermano.
Si compramos este coche, **deberemos** mucho dinero.

B. When followed by an infinitive, **deber** has various meanings according to tense and context.

1. *must, have to*[1]

   Debo acabar mi trabajo esta noche.
   Uno **debe ser** fiel.

2. *ought to, should*

   Deberíamos estar de regreso antes de medianoche.
   Deberían hacer este trabajo más rápidamente.

3. **Deber de** + infinitive expresses probability and means *must be, must have.*

   Ella no vino.   **Debe de estar** enferma.
   Llegué tarde.   Ella **debió de estar** enojada.

4. In the preterit, **deber** means *had to.*

   Debieron hacer cola en el cine.
   Debimos esperar mucho tiempo.

5. In the imperfect, **deber** denotes a repeated obligation in the past.

   Cuando era pequeño, **debía levantarme** a las seis todos los días.

---

1. **Must, to have to** may also be expressed by the constructions **tener que** + infinitive, **hay que** + infinitive, **haber de** + infinitive. (See *El verbo* **tener** *56*, and *El verbo* **haber** *24*.)

56 El verbo <u>tener</u>

A. The basic meaning of the verb **tener** is *to have, to hold, to possess.* It is never used as an auxiliary verb.

Tengo muchos deseos y poco dinero.
Teníamos una casa en el campo pero la vendimos.

B. **Tener que** + infinitive (*must, to have to*) expresses a strong obligation or necessity. (See also *El verbo* **deber** *55.*)

Tengo que trabajar.
Tenemos que salir esta noche.
Tuvieron que abandonar esta idea.

C. Idioms with **tener**

tener afición a	*to be fond of*
tener . . . años	*to be . . . years old*
tener buena cara	*to look good*
tener cara de	*to seem, to look like*
tener calma	*to be calm*
tener calor	*to be warm*
tener celos	*to be jealous*
tener cuidado	*to be careful*
tener empeño en	*to be eager to*
tener envidia	*to be envious*
tener éxito	*to be successful*
tener frío	*to be cold*
tener ganas de	*to feel like*
tener hambre	*to be hungry*
tener la culpa de	*to be to blame for*
tener la palabra	*to have the floor*
tener miedo	*to be afraid*
tener prisa	*to be in a hurry*

tener razón[1]	*to be right*
tener sed	*to be thirsty*
tener sueño	*to be sleepy*
tener suerte	*to be lucky*
tener vergüenza	*to be ashamed*

---

1. no tener razón   *to be wrong*
    estar equivocado   *to be wrong*

57 Los verbos <u>gustar</u>, <u>doler</u>, <u>faltar</u>, <u>quedar</u>

The subject of the verbs **gustar**, **doler**, **faltar**, and **quedar** is the equivalent of the English direct object, and the indirect object is the equivalent of the English subject.

Me gusta el teatro.
I like the theatre. (The theatre is pleasing to me.)

A Alicia le[1] gustaron las fotos.
Alicia liked the photos. (The photos were pleasing to Alicia.)

Le duele la cabeza.
He has a headache. (The head is hurting him.)

Me duelen las muelas.
I have a toothache. (The molars are hurting me.)

Nos falta dinero para el viaje.
We lack money for the trip. (Money is lacking to us for the trip.)

Le faltan dos dólares.
He lacks (needs) two dollars. (Two dollars are lacking to him.)

Me queda un día para terminar.
I have one day left to finish. (One day is remaining to me to finish.)

Me quedan unos minutos.
I have a few minutes left. (A few minutes are remaining to me.)

---

1. With these verbs, the object pronoun is used even when the noun appears.

58 Tablas de los verbos con cambios en la raíz

RADICAL-CHANGING VERB TYPES

INFINITIVO GERUNDIO PARTICIPIO PASIVO	INDICATIVO			
	PRESENTE	FUTURO	IMPERFECTO	PRETÉRITO
adquirir *to acquire* adquiriendo adquirido	adquiero adquieres adquiere adquirimos adquirís adquieren	adquiriré adquirirás adquirirá adquiriremos adquiriréis adquirirán	adquiría adquirías adquiría adquiríamos adquiríais adquirían	adquirí adquiriste adquirió adquirimos adquiristeis adquirieron
comenzar *to begin* comenzando comenzado	comienzo comienzas comienza comenzamos comenzáis comienzan	comenzaré comenzarás comenzará comenzaremos comenzaréis comenzarán	comenzaba comenzabas comenzaba comenzábamos comenzabais comenzaban	comencé comenzaste comenzó comenzamos comenzasteis comenzaron
concernir (def.) *to concern* concerniendo	—— —— concierne —— —— conciernen	—— —— concernerá —— —— concernerán	—— —— concernía —— —— concernían	—— —— concernió —— —— concernieron

IMPERATIVO	CONDICIONAL	SUBJUNTIVO		
		PRESENTE		IMPERFECTO
——	adquiriría	adquiera	adquiriera	adquiriese
adquiere	adquirirías	adquieras	adquirieras	adquirieses
adquiera	adquiriría	adquiera	adquiriera	adquiriese
adquiramos	adquiriríamos	adquiramos	adquiriéramos	adquiriésemos
adquirid	adquiriríais	adquiráis	adquirierais	adquirieseis
adquieran	adquirirían	adquieran	adquirieran	adquiriesen
——	comenzaría	comience	comenzara	comenzase
comienza	comenzarías	comiences	comenzaras	comenzases
comience	comenzaría	comience	comenzara	comenzase
comencemos	comenzaríamos	comencemos	comenzáramos	comenzásemos
comenzad	comenzaríais	comencéis	comenzarais	comenzaseis
comiencen	comenzarían	comiencen	comenzaran	comenzasen
——	——	——	——	——
——	concernería	concierna	concerniera	concerniese
——	——	——	——	——
——	——	——	——	——
——	concernerían	conciernan	concernieran	concerniesen

INFINITIVO GERUNDIO PARTICIPIO PASIVO	INDICATIVO			
	PRESENTE	FUTURO	IMPERFECTO	PRETÉRITO
cocer	cuezo	coceré	cocía	cocí
to cook	cueces	cocerás	cocías	cociste
	cuece	cocerá	cocía	coció
	cocemos	coceremos	cocíamos	cocimos
cociendo	cocéis	coceréis	cocíais	cocisteis
cocido	cuecen	cocerán	cocían	cocieron
confesar	confieso	confesaré	confesaba	confesé
to confess	confiesas	confesarás	confesabas	confesaste
	confiesa	confesará	confesaba	confesó
	confesamos	confesaremos	confesábamos	confesamos
confesando	confesáis	confesaréis	confesabais	confesasteis
confesado	confiesan	confesarán	confesaban	confesaron
contar	cuento	contaré	contaba	conté
to count,	cuentas	contarás	contabas	contaste
to tell	cuenta	contará	contaba	contó
	contamos	contaremos	contábamos	contamos
contando	contáis	contaréis	contabais	contasteis
contado	cuentan	contarán	contaban	contaron
corregir	corrijo	corregiré	corregía	corregí
to correct	corriges	corregirás	corregías	corregiste
	corrige	corregirá	corregía	corrigió
	corregimos	corregiremos	corregíamos	corregimos
corrigiendo	corregís	corregiréis	corregíais	corregisteis
corregido	corrigen	corregirán	corregían	corrigieron
discernir	discierno	discerniré	discernía	discerní
to discern	disciernes	discernirás	discernías	discerniste
	discierne	discernirá	discernía	discernió
	discernimos	discerniremos	discerníamos	discernimos
discerniendo	discernís	discerniréis	discerníais	discernisteis
discernido	disciernen	discernirán	discernían	discernieron

IMPERATIVO	CONDICIONAL	SUBJUNTIVO		
		PRESENTE	IMPERFECTO	
———	cocería	cueza	cociera	cociese
cuece	cocerías	cuezas	cocieras	cocieses
cueza	cocería	cueza	cociera	cociese
cozamos	coceríamos	cozamos	cociéramos	cociésemos
coced	coceríais	cozáis	cocierais	cocieseis
cuezan	cocerían	cuezan	cocieran	cociesen
———	confesaría	confiese	confesara	confesase
confiesa	confesarías	confieses	confesaras	confesases
confiese	confesaría	confiese	confesara	confesase
confesemos	confesaríamos	confesemos	confesáramos	confesásemos
confesad	confesaríais	conféséis	confesarais	confesaseis
confiesen	confesarían	confiesen	confesaran	confesasen
———	contaría	cuente	contara	contase
cuenta	contarías	cuentes	contaras	contases
cuente	contaría	cuente	contara	contase
contemos	contaríamos	contemos	contáramos	contásemos
contad	contaríais	contéis	contarais	contaseis
cuenten	contarían	cuenten	contaran	contasen
———	corregiría	corrija	corrigiera	corrigiese
corrige	corregirías	corrijas	corrigieras	corrigieses
corrija	corregiría	corrija	corrigiera	corrigiese
corrijamos	corregiríamos	corrijamos	corrigiéramos	corrigiésemos
corregid	corregiríais	corrijáis	corrigierais	corrigieseis
corrijan	corregirían	corrijan	corrigieran	corrigiesen
———	discerniría	discierna	discernía	discerní
discierne	discernirías	disciernas	discernías	discerniste
discierna	discerniría	discierna	discernía	discernió
discernamos	discerniríamos	discernamos	discerníamos	discernimos
discernid	discerniríais	discernáis	discerníais	discernisteis
disciernan	discerniría	disciernan	discernían	discernieron

INFINITIVO GERUNDIO PARTICIPIO PASIVO	INDICATIVO			
	PRESENTE	FUTURO	IMPERFECTO	PRETÉRITO
dormir	duermo	dormiré	dormía	dormí
to sleep	duermes	dormirás	dormías	dormiste
	duerme	dormirá	dormía	durmió
	dormimos	dormiremos	dormíamos	dormimos
durmiendo	dormís	dormiréis	dormíais	dormisteis
dormido	duermen	dormirán	dormían	durmieron
erguir	{irgo / yergo}	erguiré	erguía	erguí
to erect	{irgues / yergues}	erguirás	erguías	erguiste
	{irgue / yergue}	erguirá	erguía	irguió
	erguimos	erguiremos	erguíamos	erguimos
irguiendo	erguís	erguiréis	erguíais	erguisteis
erguido	{irguen / yerguen}	erguirán	erguían	irguieron
errar	yerro	erraré	erraba	erré
to err,	yerras	errarás	errabas	erraste
to make	yerra	errará	erraba	erró
a mistake	erramos	erraremos	errábamos	erramos
errando	erráis	erraréis	errabais	errasteis
errado	yerran	errarán	erraban	erraron
huir	huyo	huiré	huía	huí
to flee,	huyes	huirás	huías	huiste
to escape	huye	huirá	huía	huyó
	huimos	huiremos	huíamos	huimos
huyendo	huis	huiréis	huíais	huisteis
huido	huyen	huirán	huían	huyeron
mover	muevo	moveré	movía	moví
to move	mueves	moverás	movías	moviste
	mueve	moverá	movía	movió
	movemos	moveremos	movíamos	movimos
moviendo	movéis	moveréis	movíais	movisteis
movido	mueven	moverán	movían	movieron

IMPERATIVO	CONDICIONAL	SUBJUNTIVO		
		PRESENTE		IMPERFECTO
——	dormiría	duerma	durmiera	durmiese
duerme	dormirías	duermas	durmieras	durmieses
duerma	dormiría	duerma	durmiera	durmiese
durmamos	dormiríamos	durmamos	durmiéramos	durmiésemos
dormid	dormiríais	durmáis	durmierais	durmieseis
duerman	dormirían	duerman	durmieran	durmiesen
——	erguiría	{ irga / yerga	irguera	irguiese
{ irgue / yergue	erguirías	{ irgas / yergas	irguieras	irguieses
{ irga / yerga	erguiría	{ irga / yerga	irguiera	irguiese
irgamos	erguiríamos	irgamos	irguiéramos	irguiésemos
erguid	erguiríais	irgáis	irguierais	irguieseis
{ irgan / yergan	erguirían	{ irgan / yergan	irguieran	irguiesen
——	erraría	yerre	errara	errase
yerra	errarías	yerres	erraras	errases
yerre	erraría	yerre	errara	errase
erremos	erraríamos	erremos	erráramos	errásemos
errad	erraríais	erréis	errarais	erraseis
yerren	errarían	yerren	erraran	errasen
——	huiría	huya	huyera	huyese
huye	huirías	huyas	huyeras	huyeses
huya	huiría	huya	huyera	huyese
huyamos	huiríamos	huyamos	huyéramos	huyésemos
huid	huiríais	huyáis	huyerais	huyeseis
huyan	huirían	huyan	huyeran	huyesen
——	movería	mueva	moviera	moviese
mueve	moverías	muevas	movieras	movieses
mueva	movería	mueva	moviera	moviese
movamos	moveríamos	movamos	moviéramos	moviésemos
moved	moveríais	mováis	movierais	movieseis
muevan	moverían	muevan	movieran	moviesen

INFINITIVO GERUNDIO PARTICIPIO PASIVO	INDICATIVO			
	PRESENTE	FUTURO	IMPERFECTO	PRETÉRITO
oler	**hue**lo	oleré	olía	olí
to smell	**hue**les	olerás	olías	oliste
	huele	olerá	olía	olió
	olemos	oleremos	olíamos	olimos
oliendo	oléis	oleréis	olíais	olisteis
olido	**hue**len	olerán	olían	olieron
pedir	pido	pediré	pedía	pedí
to ask (for)	pides	pedirás	pedías	pediste
	pide	pedirá	pedía	pidió
	pedimos	pediremos	pedíamos	pedimos
pidiendo	pedís	pediréis	pedíais	pedisteis
pedido	piden	pedirán	pedían	pidieron
reír	**rí**o	reiré	reía	reí
to laugh	**rí**es	reirás	reías	reíste
	ríe	reirá	reía	**rió**
	reímos	reiremos	reíamos	reíamos
riendo	reís	reiréis	reíais	reísteis
reído	**rí**en	reirán	reían	**rieron**
sentir	siento	sentiré	sentía	sentí
to feel;	sientes	sentirás	sentías	sentiste
to regret	siente	sentirá	sentía	sintió
	sentimos	sentiremos	sentíamos	sentimos
sintiendo	sentís	sentiréis	sentíais	sentisteis
sentido	sienten	sentirán	sentían	sintieron
tender	tiendo	tenderé	tendía	tendí
to tend;	tiendes	tenderás	tendías	tendiste
to stretch	tiende	tenderá	tendía	tendió
	tendemos	tenderemos	tendíamos	tendimos
tendiendo	tendéis	tenderéis	tendíais	tendisteis
tendido	tienden	tenderán	tendían	tendieron

IMPERATIVO	CONDICIONAL	SUBJUNTIVO		
		PRESENTE	IMPERFECTO	
――	olería	**hue**la	oliera	oliese
huele	olerías	**hue**las	olieras	olieses
huela	olería	**hue**la	oliera	oliese
olamos	oleríamos	olamos	oliéramos	oliésemos
oled	oleríais	oláis	olierais	olieseis
huelan	olerían	**hue**lan	olieran ·	oliesen
――	pediría	pida	pidiera	pidiese
pide	pedirías	pidas	pidieras	pidieses
pida	pediría	pida	pidiera	pidiese
pidamos	pediríamos	pidamos	pidiéramos	pidiésemos
pedid	pediríais	pidáis	pidierais	pidieseis
pidan	pedirían	pidan	pidieran	pidiesen
――	reiría	**rí**a	**ri**era	**ri**ese
ríe	reirías	**rí**as	**ri**eras	**ri**eses
ría	reiría	**rí**a	**ri**era	**ri**ese
riamos	reiríamos	**ri**amos	**ri**éramos	**ri**ésemos
reíd	reiríais	**ri**áis	**ri**erais	**ri**eseis
rían	reirían	**rí**an	**ri**eran	**ri**esen
――	sentiría	sienta	sintiera	sintiese
siente	sentirías	sientas	sintieras	sintieses
sienta	sentiría	sienta	sintiera	sintiese
sintamos	sentiríamos	sintamos	sintiéramos	sintiésemos
sentid	sentiríais	sitáis	sintierais	sintieseis
sientan	sentirían	sientan	sintieran	sintiesen
――	tendería	tienda	tendiera	tendiese
tiende	tenderías	tiendas	tendieras	tendieses
tienda	tendería	tienda	tendiera	tendiese
tendamos	tenderíamos	tendamos	tendiéramos	tendiésemos
tended	tenderíais	tendáis	tendierais	tendieseis
tiendan	tenderían	tiendan	tendieran	tendiesen

INFINITIVO GERUNDIO PARTICIPIO PASIVO	INDICATIVO			
	PRESENTE	FUTURO	IMPERFECTO	PRETÉRITO
teñir	tiño	teñiré	teñía	teñí
to dye	tiñes	teñirás	teñías	teñiste
	tiñe	teñirá	teñía	**tiñó**
	teñimos	teñiremos	teñíamos	teñimos
tiñendo	teñís	teñiréis	teñíais	teñisteis
teñido	tiñen	teñirán	teñían	**tiñeron**
torcer	**tu**erzo	torceré	torcía	torcí
to twist	**tu**erces	torcerás	torcías	torciste
	tuerce	torcerá	torcía	torció
	torcemos	torceremos	torcíamos	torcimos
torciendo	torcéis	torceréis	torcíais	torcisteis
torcido	**tu**ercen	torcerán	torcían	torcieron
volver	**vu**elvo	volveré	volvía	volví
to return,	**vu**elves	volverás	volvías	volviste
to turn	**vu**elve	volverá	volvía	volvió
	volvemos	volveremos	volvíamos	volvimos
volviendo	volvéis	volveréis	volvíais	volvisteis
vuelto	**vu**elven	volverán	volvían	volvieron

IMPERATIVO	CONDICIONAL	SUBJUNTIVO		
		PRESENTE		IMPERFECTO
——	teñiría	tiña	tiñera	tiñese
tiñe	teñirías	tiñas	tiñeras	tiñeses
tiña	teñiría	tiña	tiñera	tiñese
tiñamos	teñiríamos	tiñamos	tiñéramos	tiñésemos
teñid	teñiríais	tiñáis	tiñerais	tiñeseis
tiñan	teñirían	tiñan	tiñeran	tiñesen
——	torcería	tuerza	torciera	torciese
tuerce	torcerías	tuerzas	torcieras	torcieses
tuerza	torcería	tuerza	torciera	torciese
torzamos	torceríamos	torzamos	torciéramos	torciésemos
torced	torceríais	torzáis	torcierais	torcieseis
tuerzan	torcerían	tuerzan	torcieran	torciesen
——	volvería	vuelva	volviera	volviese
vuelve	volverías	vuelvas	volvieras	volvieses
vuelva	volvería	vuelva	volviera	volviese
volvamos	volveríamos	volvamos	volviéramos	volviésemos
volved	volveríais	volváis	volvierais	volvieseis
vuelvan	volverían	vuelvan	volvieran	volviesen

59

Tablas de los verbos irregulares

INFINITIVO GERUNDIO PARTICIPIO PASIVO	INDICATIVO			
	PRESENTE	FUTURO	IMPERFECTO	PRETÉRITO
abolir (def.)	———	aboliré	abolía	abolí
to abolish	———	abolirás	abolías	aboliste
	———	abolirá	abolía	abolió
	abolimos	aboliremos	abolíamos	abolimos
aboliendo	abolís	aboliréis	abolíais	abolisteis
abolido	———	abolirán	abolían	abolieron
andar	ando	andaré	andaba	**anduve**
to walk	andas	andarás	andabas	**anduviste**
	anda	andará	andaba	**anduvo**
	andamos	andaremos	andábamos	**anduvimos**
andando	andáis	andaréis	andabais	**anduvisteis**
andado	andan	andarán	andaban	**anduvieron**
asir	as**g**o	asiré	asía	así
to seize	ases	asirás	asías	asiste
	ase	asirá	asía	asió
	asimos	asiremos	asíamos	asimos
asiendo	asís	asiréis	asíais	asisteis
asido	asen	asirán	asían	asieron
caber	**quep**o	**cabr**é	cabía	**cupe**
to fit in,	cabes	**cabr**ás	cabías	**cupiste**
to be	cabe	**cabr**á	cabía	**cupo**
contained in	cabemos	**cabr**emos	cabíamos	**cupimos**
cabiendo	cabéis	**cabr**éis	cabíais	**cupisteis**
cabido	caben	**cabr**án	cabían	**cupieron**

IMPERATIVO	CONDICIONAL	SUBJUNTIVO		
		PRESENTE	IMPERFECTO	
——	aboliría	——	aboliera	aboliese
——	abolirías	——	abolieras	abolieses
——	aboliría	——	aboliera	aboliese
——	aboliríamos	——	aboliéramos	aboliésemos
abolid	aboliríais	——	abolierais	abolieseis
——	abolirían	——	abolieran	aboliesen
——	andaría	ande	**anduv**iera	**anduv**iese
anda	andarías	andes	**anduv**ieras	**anduv**ieses
ande	andaría	ande	**anduv**iera	**anduv**iese
andemos	andaríamos	andemos	**anduv**iéramos	**anduv**iésemos
andad	andaríais	andéis	**anduv**ierais	**anduv**ieseis
anden	andarían	anden	**anduv**ieran	**anduv**iesen
——	asiría	asga	asiera	asiese
ase	asirías	asgas	asieras	asieses
asga	asiría	asga	asiera	asiese
asgamos	asiríamos	asgamos	asiéramos	asiésemos
asid	asiríais	asgáis	asierais	asieseis
asgan	asirían	asgan	asieran	asiesen
——	**cabr**ía	**quep**a	**cup**iera	**cup**iese
cabe	**cabr**ías	**quep**as	**cup**ieras	**cup**ieses
quepa	**cabr**ía	**quep**a	**cup**iera	**cup**iese
quepamos	**cabr**íamos	**quep**amos	**cup**iéramos	**cup**iésemos
cabed	**cabr**íais	**quep**áis	**cup**ierais	**cup**ieseis
quepan	**cabr**ían	**quep**an	**cup**ieran	**cup**iesen

INFINITIVO GERUNDIO PARTICIPIO PASIVO	INDICATIVO			
	PRESENTE	FUTURO	IMPERFECTO	PRETÉRITO
caer	**cai**go	caeré	caía	caí
to fall	caes	caerás	caías	caíste
	cae	caerá	caía	cayó
	caemos	caeremos	caíamos	caímos
cayendo	caéis	caeréis	caíais	caísteis
caído	caen	caerán	caían	cayeron
conducir	conduzco	conduciré	conducía	**conduje**
to conduct	conduces	conducirás	conducías	**conduj**iste
	conduce	conducirá	conducía	**conduj**o
	conducimos	conduciremos	conducíamos	**conduj**imos
conduciendo	conducís	conduciréis	conducíais	**conduj**isteis
conducido	conducen	conducirán	conducían	**conduj**eron
conocer	conozco	conoceré	conocía	conocí
to know	conoces	conocerás	conocías	conociste
	conoce	conocerá	conocía	conoció
	conocemos	conoceremos	conocíamos	conocimos
conociendo	conocéis	conoceréis	conocíais	conocisteis
conocido	conocen	conocerán	conocían	conocieron
dar	doy	daré	daba	di
to give	das	darás	dabas	diste
	da	dará	daba	dio
	damcs	daremos	dábamos	dimos
dando	dais	daréis	dabais	disteis
dado	dan	darán	daban	dieron
decir	**dig**o	**dir**é	decía	**dij**e
to say,	dices	**dir**ás	decías	**dij**iste
to tell	dice	**dir**á	decía	**dij**o
	decimos	**dir**emos	decíamos	**dij**imos
diciendo	decís	**dir**éis	decíais	**dij**isteis
dicho	dicen	**dir**án	decían	**dij**eron

IMPERATIVO	CONDICIONAL	SUBJUNTIVO		
		PRESENTE		IMPERFECTO
——	caería	caiga	cayera	cayese
cae	caerías	caigas	cayeras	cayeses
caiga	caería	caiga	cayera	cayese
caigamos	caeríamos	caigamos	cayéramos	cayésemos
caed	caeríais	caigáis	cayerais	cayeseis
caigan	caerían	caigan	cayeran	cayesen
——	conduciría	conduzca	condujera	condujese
conduce	conducirías	conduzcas	condujeras	condujeses
conduzca	conduciría	conduzca	condujera	condujese
conduzcamos	conduciríamos	conduzcamos	condujéramos	condujésemos
conducid	conduciríais	conduzcáis	condujerais	condujeseis
conduzcan	conducirían	conduzcan	condujeran	condujesen
——	conocería	conozca	conociera	conociese
conoce	conocerías	conozcas	conocieras	conocieses
conozca	conocería	conozca	conociera	conociese
conozcamos	conoceríamos	conozcamos	conociéramos	conociésemos
conoced	conoceríais	conozcáis	conocierais	conocieseis
conozcan	conocerían	conozcan	conocieran	conociesen
——	daría	dé	diera	diese
da	darías	des	dieras	dieses
dé	daría	dé	diera	diese
demos	daríamos	demos	diéramos	diésemos
dad	daríais	deis	dierais	dieseis
den	darían	den	dieran	diesen
——	diría	diga	dijera	dijese
di	dirías	digas	dijeras	dijeses
diga	diría	diga	dijera	dijese
digamos	diríamos	digamos	dijéramos	dijésemos
decid	diríais	digáis	dijerais	dijeseis
digan	dirían	digan	dijeran	dijesen

INFINITIVO GERUNDIO PARTICIPIO PASIVO	INDICATIVO			
	PRESENTE	FUTURO	IMPERFECTO	PRETÉRITO
estar	estoy	estaré	estaba	**estuve**
to be	estás	estarás	estabas	**estuviste**
	está	estará	estaba	**estuvo**
	estamos	estaremos	estábamos	**estuvimos**
estando	estáis	estaréis	estabais	**estuvisteis**
estado	están	estarán	estaban	**estuvieron**
haber	**he**	**habré**	había	**hube**
to have	**has**	**habrás**	habías	**hub**iste
	ha	**habrá**	había	**hubo**
	hemos	**habremos**	habíamos	**hub**imos
habiendo	habéis	**habréis**	habíais	**hub**isteis
habido	**han**	**habrán**	habían	**hub**ieron
hacer	hago	**haré**	hacía	**hice**
to do;	haces	**harás**	hacías	**hic**iste
to make	hace	**hará**	hacía	**hizo**
	hacemos	**haremos**	hacíamos	**hic**imos
haciendo	hacéis	**haréis**	hacíais	**hic**isteis
hecho	hacen	**harán**	hacían	**hic**ieron
ir	**voy**	iré	**iba**	**fui**
to go	vas	irás	**ibas**	**fuiste**
	va	irá	**iba**	**fue**
	vamos	iremos	**íbamos**	**fuimos**
yendo	vais	iréis	**ibais**	**fuisteis**
ido	van	irán	**iban**	**fueron**
lucir	luzco	luciré	lucía	lucí
to shine;	luces	lucirás	lucías	luciste
to show off	luce	lucirá	lucía	lució
	lucimos	luciremos	lucíamos	lucimos
luciendo	lucís	luciréis	lucíais	lucisteis
lucido	lucen	lucirán	lucían	lucieron

IMPERATIVO	CONDICIONAL	SUBJUNTIVO		
		PRESENTE	IMPERFECTO	
——	estaría	esté	estuviera	estuviese
está	estarías	estés	estuvieras	estuvieses
esté	estaría	esté	estuviera	estuviese
estemos	estaríamos	estemos	estuviéramos	estuviésemos
estad	estaríais	estéis	estuvierais	estuvieseis
estén	estarían	estén	estuvieran	estuviesen
——	habría	haya	hubiera	hubiese
——	habrías	hayas	hubieras	hubieses
——	habría	haya	hubiera	hubiese
——	habríamos	hayamos	hubiéramos	hubiésemos
——	habríais	hayáis	hubierais	hubieseis
——	habrían	hayan	hubieran	hubiesen
——	haría	haga	hiciera	hiciese
haz	harías	hagas	hicieras	hicieses
haga	haría	haga	hiciera	hiciese
hagamos	haríamos	hagamos	hiciéramos	hiciésemos
haced	haríais	hagáis	hicierais	hicieseis
hagan	harían	hagan	hicieran	hiciesen
——	iría	vaya	fuera	fuese
ve	irías	vayas	fueras	fueses
vaya	iría	vaya	fuera	fuese
vayamos	iríamos	vayamos	fuéramos	fuésemos
id	iríais	vayáis	fuerais	fueseis
vayan	irían	vayan	fueran	fuesen
——	luciría	luzca	luciera	luciese
luce	lucirías	luzcas	lucieras	lucieses
luzca	luciría	luzca	luciera	luciese
luzcamos	luciríamos	luzcamos	luciéramos	luciésemos
lucid	luciríais	luzcáis	lucierais	lucieseis
luzcan	lucirían	luzcan	lucieran	luciesen

INFINITIVO GERUNDIO PARTICIPIO PASIVO	INDICATIVO			
	PRESENTE	FUTURO	IMPERFECTO	PRETÉRITO
nacer to be born naciendo nacido	nazco naces nace nacemos nacéis nacen	naceré nacerás nacerá naceremos naceréis nacerán	nacía nacías nacía nacíamos nacíais nacían	nací naciste nació nacimos nacisteis nacieron
oír to hear oyendo oído	oigo oyes oye oímos oís oyen	oiré oirás oirá oiremos oiréis oirán	oía oías oía oíamos oíais oían	oí oíste oyó oímos oísteis oyeron
parecer to appear, to seem pareciendo parecido	parezco pareces parece parecemos parecéis parecen	pareceré parecerás parecerá pareceremos pareceréis parecerán	parecía parecías parecía parecíamos parecíais parecían	parecí pareciste pareció parecimos parecisteis parecieron
placer to please placiendo placido	plazco places place placemos placéis placen	placeré placerás placerá placeremos placeréis placerán	placía placías placía placíamos placíais placían	plací placiste { plació **plugo** placimos placisteis placieron
poder to be able, can pudiendo podido	puedo puedes puede podemos podéis pueden	**podré** **podrás** **podrá** **podremos** **podréis** **podrán**	podía podías podía podíamos podíais podían	**pude** **pud**iste **pudo** **pud**imos **pud**isteis **pud**ieron

IMPERATIVO	CONDICIONAL	SUBJUNTIVO		
		PRESENTE		IMPERFECTO
____	nacería	nazca	naciera	naciese
nace	nacerías	nazcas	nacieras	nacieses
nazca	nacería	nazca	naciera	naciese
nazcamos	naceríamos	nazcamos	naciéramos	naciésemos
naced	naceríais	nazcáis	nacierais	nacieseis
nazcan	nacerían	nazcan	nacieran	naciesen
____	oiría	oiga	oyera	oyese
oye	oirías	oigas	oyeras	oyeses
oiga	oiría	oiga	oyera	oyese
oigamos	oiríamos	oigamos	oyéramos	oyésemos
oíd	oiríais	oigáis	oyerais	oyeseis
oigan	oirían	oigan	oyeran	oysen
____	parecería	parezca	pareciera	pareciese
parece	parecerías	parezcas	parecieras	parecieses
parezca	parecería	parezca	pareciera	pareciese
parezcamos	pareceríamos	parezcamos	pareciéramos	pareciésemos
pareced	pareceríais	parezcáis	parecierais	parecieseis
parezcan	parecerían	parezcan	parecieran	pareciesen
____	placería	plazca	placiera	placiese
place	placerías	plazcas	placieras	placieses
plazca	placería	plazca	{ placiera / pluguiera	{ placiese / pluguiese
plazcamos	placeríamos	plazcamos	placiéramos	placiésemos
placed	placeríais	plazcáis	placierais	placieseis
plazcan	placerían	plazcan	placieran	placiesen
____	podría	pueda	pudiera	pudiese
puede	podrías	puedas	pudieras	pudieses
pueda	podría	pueda	pudiera	pudiese
podamos	podríamos	podamos	pudiéramos	pudiésemos
poded	podríais	podáis	pudierais	pudieseis
puedan	podrían	puedan	pudieran	pudiesen

INFINITIVO GERUNDIO PARTICIPIO PASIVO	INDICATIVO			
	PRESENTE	FUTURO	IMPERFECTO	PRETÉRITO
poner	pongo	**pondré**	ponía	**puse**
to put,	pones	**pondrás**	ponías	**pusiste**
to place	pone	**pondrá**	ponía	**puso**
	ponemos	**pondremos**	poníamos	**pusimos**
poniendo	ponéis	**pondréis**	poníais	**pusisteis**
puesto	ponen	**pondrán**	ponían	**pusieron**
querer	quiero	**querré**	quería	**quise**
to want,	quieres	**querrás**	querías	**quisiste**
to wish;	quiere	**querrá**	quería	**quiso**
to love	queremos	**querremos**	queríamos	**quisimos**
queriendo	queréis	**querréis**	queríais	**quisisteis**
querido	quieren	**querrán**	querían	**quisieron**
saber	sé	**sabré**	sabía	**supe**
to know	sabes	**sabrás**	sabías	**supiste**
	sabe	**sabrá**	sabía	**supo**
	sabemos	**sabremos**	sabíamos	**supimos**
sabiendo	sabéis	**sabréis**	sabíais	**supisteis**
sabido	saben	**sabrán**	sabían	**supieron**
salir	salgo	**saldré**	salía	salí
to leave,	sales	**saldrás**	salías	saliste
to go out	sale	**saldrá**	salía	salió
	salimos	**saldremos**	salíamos	salimos
saliendo	salís	**saldréis**	salíais	salisteis
salido	salen	**saldrán**	salían	salieron

IMPERATIVO	CONDICIONAL	SUBJUNTIVO		
		PRESENTE		IMPERFECTO
____	pondría	ponga	pusiera	pusiese
pon	pondrías	pongas	pusieras	pusieses
ponga	pondría	ponga	pusiera	pusiese
pongamos	pondríamos	pongamos	pusiéramos	pusiésemos
poned	pondríais	pongáis	pusierais	pusieseis
pongan	pondrían	pongan	pusieran	pusiesen
____	querría	quiera	quisiera	quisiese
quiere	querrías	quieras	quisieras	quisieses
quiera	querría	quiera	quisiera	quisiese
queramos	querríamos	queramos	quisiéramos	quisiésemos
quered	querrías	queráis	quisierais	quisieseis
quieran	querrían	quieran	quisieran	quisiesen
____	sabría	sepa	supiera	supiese
sabe	sabrías	sepas	supieras	supieses
sepa	sabría	sepa	supiera	supiese
sepamos	sabríamos	sepamos	supiéramos	supiésemos
sabed	sabríais	sepáis	supierais	supieseis
sepan	sabrían	sepan	supieran	supiesen
____	saldría	salga	saliera	saliese
sal	saldrías	salgas	salieras	salieses
salga	saldría	salga	saliera	saliese
salgamos	saldríamos	salgamos	saliéramos	saliésemos
salid	saldríais	salgáis	salierais	salieseis
salgan	saldrían	salgan	salieran	saliesen

INFINITIVO GERUNDIO PARTICIPIO PASIVO	INDICATIVO			
	PRESENTE	FUTURO	IMPERFECTO	PRETÉRITO
satisfacer *to satisfy* satisfaciendo **satisfecho**	satisfago satisfaces satisface satisfacemos satisfacéis satisfacen	**satisfaré** **satisfarás** **satisfará** **satisfaremos** **satisfaréis** **satisfarán**	satisfacía satisfacías satisfacía satisfacíamos satisfacíais satisfacían	**satisfice** **satisficiste** **satisfizo** **satisficimos** **satisficisteis** **satisficieron**
ser *to be* siendo sido	**soy** **eres** **es** **somos** **sois** **son**	seré serás será seremos seréis serán	**era** **eras** **era** **éramos** **erais** **eran**	**fui** **fuiste** **fue** **fuimos** **fuisteis** **fueron**
tener *to have* teniendo tenido	tengo tienes tiene tenemos tenéis tienen	**tendré** **tendrás** **tendrá** **tendremos** **tendréis** **tendrán**	tenía tenías tenía teníamos teníais tenían	**tuve** **tuviste** **tuvo** **tuvimos** **tuvisteis** **tuvieron**
traer *to bring* trayendo traído	**traigo** traes trae traemos traéis traen	traeré traerás traerá traeremos traeréis traerán	traía traías traía traíamos traíais traían	**traje** **trajiste** **trajo** **trajimos** **trajisteis** **trajeron**

IMPERATIVO	CONDICIONAL	SUBJUNTIVO		
		PRESENTE	IMPERFECTO	
satisfaz	satisfaría	satisfaga	satisficiera	satisficiese
satisface	satisfarías	satisfagas	satisficieras	satisficieses
satisfaga	satisfaría	satisfaga	satisficiera	satisficiese
satisfagamos	satisfaríamos	satisfagamos	satisficiéramos	satisficiésemos
satisfaced	satisfaríais	satisfagáis	satisficierais	satisficieseis
satifagan	satisfarían	satisfagan	satisficieran	satisficiesen
____	sería	sea	fuera	fuese
sé	serías	seas	fueras	fueses
sea	sería	sea	fuera	fuese
seamos	seríamos	seamos	fuéramos	fuésemos
sed	seríais	seáis	fuerais	fueseis
sean	serían	sean	fueran	fuesen
____	tendría	tenga	tuviera	tuviese
ten	tendrías	tengas	tuvieras	tuvieses
tenga	tendría	tenga	tuviera	tuviese
tengamos	tendríamos	tengamos	tuviéramos	tuviésemos
tened	tendríais	tengáis	tuvierais	tuvieseis
tengan	tendrían	tengan	tuvieran	tuviesen
____	traería	traiga	trajera	trajese
trae	traerías	traigas	trajeras	trajeses
traiga	traería	traiga	trajera	trajese
traigamos	traeríamos	traigamos	trajéramos	trajésemos
traed	traeríais	traigáis	trajerais	trajeseis
traigan	traerían	traigan	trajeran	trajesen

INFINITIVO GERUNDIO PARTICIPIO PASIVO	INDICATIVO			
	PRESENTE	FUTURO	IMPERFECTO	PRETÉRITO
valer	valgo	**valdré**	valía	valí
to be worth	vales	**valdrás**	valías	valiste
	vale	**valdrá**	valía	valió
	valemos	**valdremos**	valíamos	valimos
valiendo	valéis	**valdréis**	valíais	valisteis
valido	valen	**valdrán**	valían	valieron
venir	vengo	**vendré**	venía	**vine**
to come	vienes	**vendrás**	venías	**vin**iste
	viene	**vendrá**	venía	**vino**
	venimos	**vendremos**	veníamos	**vin**imos
viniendo	venís	**vendréis**	veníais	**vin**isteis
venido	vienen	**vendrán**	venían	**vin**ieron
ver	veo	veré	veía	vi
to see	ves	verás	veías	viste
	ve	verá	veía	vio
	vemos	veremos	veíamos	vimos
viendo	veis	veréis	veíais	visteis
visto	ven	verán	veían	vieron

IMPERATIVO	CONDICIONAL	SUBJUNTIVO		
		PRESENTE	IMPERFECTO	
——	valdría	valga	valiera	valiese
val	valdrías	valgas	valieras	valieses
valga	valdría	valga	valiera	valiese
valgamos	valdríamos	valgamos	valiéramos	valiésemos
valed	valdríais	valgáis	valierais	valieseis
valgan	valdrían	valgan	valieran	valiesen
——	vendría	venga	viniera	viniese
ven	vendrías	vengas	vinieras	vinieses
venga	vendría	venga	viniera	viniese
vengamos	vendríamos	vengamos	viniéramos	viniésemos
venid	vendríais	vengáis	vinierais	vinieseis
vengan	vendrían	vengan	vinieran	viniesen
——	vería	vea	viera	viese
ve	verías	veas	vieras	vieses
vea	vería	vea	viera	viese
veamos	veríamos	veamos	viéramos	viésemos
ved	veríais	veáis	vierais	vieseis
vean	verían	vean	vieran	viesen

Lista de los verbos irregulares y de los verbos con cambios
60 en la raíz

INFINITIVE	VERB TYPE	INFINITIVE	VERB TYPE
abastecer	parecer	amanecer *(imp.)*[2]	parecer
aborrecer	parecer	anochecer *(imp.)*	parecer
absolver	volver	antedecir	decir
abstenerse	tener	anteponer	poner
abstraer	traer	aparecer	parecer
acaecer *(def.)*[1]	parecer	apetecer	parecer
acertar	comenzar	apostar	contar
acontecer *(def.)*	parecer	apretar	comenzar
acordar	contar	aprobar	contar
acostar	contar	argüir	huir
acrecer	nacer	arrendar	comenzar
adestrar ⎱ adiestrar ⎰	comenzar	arrepentirse	sentir
		ascender	tender
adherir	sentir	asentar	comenzar
adolecer	parecer	asentir	sentir
adormecer	parecer	aserrar	comenzar
advenir	venir	asolar	contar
advertir	sentir	astreñir	teñir
aferrar	comenzar	atender	tender
afluir	huir	atenerse	tener
agradecer	parecer	atraer	traer
aguerrir *(def.)*	abolir *(def.)*	atravesar	confesar
alentar	comenzar	atribuir	huir
almorzar	contar	avenir	venir

1. *(def.)* A defective verb lacking some of the usual grammatical forms.
2. *(imp.)* A verb used only in the third person singular.

[222]

INFINITIVE	VERB TYPE	INFINITIVE	VERB TYPE
aventar	comenzar	contener	tener
avergonzar(se)	contar	contradecir	decir
balbucir *(def.)*	abolir *(def.)*	contraer	traer
bendecir[3]	decir	contribuir	huir
blandir *(def.)*	abolir *(def.)*	convalecer	parecer
calentar	comenzar	convenir	venir
carecer	parecer	convertir	sentir
cegar	comenzar	costar	contar
ceñir	teñir	crecer	parecer
cerrar	comenzar	decaer	caer
cimentar	comenzar	decrecer	parecer
colar	contar	deducir	conducir
colgar	contar	defender	tender
compadecer	conocer	deferir	sentir
comparecer	parecer	demostrar	contar
competir	pedir	denegar	comenzar
complacer	placer[4]	deponer	poner
componer	poner	derretir	pedir
comprobar	contar	desacertar	comenzar
concebir	pedir	desacordar	contar
concertar	comenzar	desagradecer	parecer
concluir	huir	desalentar	comenzar
concordar	contar	desaparecer	parecer
condescender	tender	desapretar	comenzar
conferir	sentir	desaprobar	contar
confesar	comenzar	desatender	tender
confluir	huir	descender	tender
conmover	mover	descolgar	contar
conseguir	pedir	descomponer	poner
consentir	sentir	desconcertar	comenzar
consolar	contar	desconocer	conocer
constituir	huir	desconsolar	contar
constreñir	teñir	descontar	contar
construir	huir	desconvenir	venir
contender	tender	desenterrar	comenzar

---

3. See *El participio pasivo 33.1C.*
4. The irregular forms **plugo, pluguiera,** and **pluguiese** are not used in compounds of **placer.**

INFINITIVE	VERB TYPE	INFINITIVE	VERB TYPE
desentumecer	parecer	empobrecer	parecer
desenvolver	volver	enardecer	parecer
desfallecer	parecer	encandecer	parecer
desfavorecer	parecer	encanecer	parecer
deshacer	hacer	encender	tender
desherbar	comenzar	encerrar	comenzar
desmembrar	comenzar	encomendar	comenzar
desmentir	sentir	endurecer	parecer
desmerecer	parecer	enflaquecer	parecer
desobedecer	parecer	enfurecer	parecer
despedir	pedir	engrandecer	parecer
despertar	comenzar	enmohecer	parecer
desplacer	placer[4]	enorgullecer	parecer
desplegar	comenzar	enriquecer	parecer
desteñir	teñir	enrodar	contar
desterrar	comenzar	enrojecer	parecer
destituir	huir	ensangrentar	contar
destruir	huir	ensordecer	parecer
desvanecer	parecer	entender	tender
desvestir	pedir	enterrar	comenzar
detener	tener	entorpecer	parecer
devenir	venir	entrecerrar	comenzar
devolver	volver	entretener	tener
diferir	sentir	entrever	ver
digerir	sentir	entristecer	parecer
diluir	huir	entumecer	parecer
disminuir	huir	envejecer	parecer
disolver	volver	envolver	volver
distraer	traer	equivaler	valer
distribuir	huir	escarmentar	comenzar
divertir	sentir	encarnecer	parecer
doler	volver	esclarecer	parecer
elegir	corregir	establecer	parecer
embellecer	parecer	estremecer	parecer
emblandecer	parecer	estreñir	teñir
emblanquecer	parecer	excluir	huir
embrutecer	parecer	expedir	pedir
empedernir *(def.)*	abolir *(def.)*	exponer	poner
empezar	comenzar	extender	tender

INFINITIVE	VERB TYPE	INFINITIVE	VERB TYPE
extraer	traer	nevar *(imp.)*	comenzar
fallecer	parecer	obedecer	parecer
favorecer	parecer	obstruir	huir
florecer	parecer	obtener	tener
fortalecer	parecer	oponer	poner
forzar	contar	oscurecer	parecer
fregar	comenzar	padecer	parecer
freír	reír	pensar	comenzar
gemir	pedir	perder	tender
gobernar	comenzar	perecer	parecer
helar	comenzar	permanecer	parecer
herir	sentir	perseguir	pedir
hervir	sentir	pertenecer	parecer
impedir	pedir	pervertir	sentir
incluir	huir	plegar	comenzar
inducir	conducir	poblar	contar
influir	huir	posponer	poner
ingerir	sentir	predecir	decir
inquirir	adquirir	predisponer	poner
instruir	huir	preferir	sentir
interponer	poner	presentir	sentir
intervenir	venir	prevalecer	parecer
introducir	conducir	prevenir	venir
invertir	sentir	prever	ver
jugar	contar	probar	contar
llover *(imp.)*	volver	producir	conducir
maldecir	decir	proponer	poner
manifestar	comenzar	quebrar	comenzar
mantener	tener	reaparecer	parecer
medir	pedir	recaer	caer
melar	comenzar	recomendar	comenzar
mentir	sentir	reconstituir	huir
merecer	parecer	reconstruir	huir
merendar	comenzar	recordar	contar
moler	volver	recostar	contar
morder	mover	reducir	conducir
morir	dormir	referir	sentir
mostrar	contar	reforzar	contar
negar	comenzar	regar	comenzar

INFINITIVE	VERB TYPE	INFINITIVE	VERB TYPE
rejuvenecer	parecer	servir	pedir
relucir	lucir	sobrentender	tender
remendar	comenzar	sobreponer	poner
renacer	nacer	sobresalir	salir
rendir	pedir	soldar	contar
renegar	comenzar	soler (def.)	mover
renovar	contar	soltar	contar
reñir	teñir	sonar	contar
repetir	pedir	soñar	contar
reponer	poner	sostener	tener
reprobar	contar	sustituir	huir
requerir	sentir	substraer	traer
resentirse	sentir	subvenir	venir
resolver	volver	sugerir	sentir
resplandecer	parecer	suponer	poner
restablecer	parecer	temblar	comenzar
restituir	huir	tentar	comenzar
retorcer	torcer	tostar	contar
retribuir	huir	traducir	conducir
reventar	comenzar	transferir	sentir
revolcar	contar	transponer	poner
revolver	volver	tropezar	comenzar
seducir	conducir	vestir	pedir
seguir	pedir	volar	contar
sentar	comenzar	volcar	contar
serrar	comenzar		

Nomenclatura
61 gramatical

ADJECTIVE: (el) adjetivo

A descriptive, qualifying, or limiting word modifying a noun.

ADVERB: (el) adverbio

A word which modifies a verb, an adjective, or another adverb.

ANTECEDENT: (el) antecedente

The word, phrase, or clause previously mentioned to which a pronoun refers.

ARTICLE: (el) artículo

The word placed before a noun reflecting its gender and indicating if it is definite or indefinite.

AUXILIARY VERB: (el) verbo auxiliar

A verb which helps to form a tense.
haber + past participle: compound tenses
estar + present participle: progressive tenses
acabar de + infinitive: recent past
ir a + infinitive: near future

CAPITAL LETTER: (la) mayúscula

CLAUSE: (la) oración, (la) cláusula

Any group of words containing a subject and a predicate.
dependent: subordinada
main (principal): principal

COMPOUND TENSE: (el) tiempo compuesto

A verbal phrase composed of a conjugated auxiliary verb and a past participle of a second verb.

CONDITIONAL: (el) condicional (potencial)

CONJUNCTION: la conjunción

A word used to link words, phrases, or clauses.

CONSONANT: (la) consonante

DASH: (la) raya

DEMONSTRATIVE: demostrativo

A word which indicates or points out the person or the thing referred to.

DIAERESIS: (la) diéresis

DIRECT OBJECT: (el) objeto directo

A noun or pronoun receiving the action of a transitive verb. A direct object answers the questions "what? " or "whom? "

Yo tengo **el libro**.   Yo **lo** tengo.

ENDING: (la) terminación

GENDER: (el) género

The masculine or feminine property of nouns and pronouns.

GERUND: In English, a noun which is formed from a verb and has the ending **-ing**. In Spanish, the infinitive is used instead.

Smoking is bad for the health.   **El fumar** es malo para la salud.

HYPHEN: (el) guión

IDIOM: (el) modismo

A set expression which has a meaning different from the literal or which is contrary to the usual patterns of the language.

IMPERATIVE: (el) imperativo

The form of the verb that expresses a command or a request.

IMPERFECT: (el) imperfecto

INDICATIVE: (el) indicativo

INDIRECT OBJECT: (el) objeto indirecto

A noun or pronoun receiving the action of a verb indirectly. An indirect object indicates to whom or to what the action is done.

Escribí a mi madre.   **Le** escribí.

INFINITIVE: **(el) infinitivo**

The form of the verb that expresses the general meaning of the verb without regard to person, number, or time.

INTRANSITIVE VERB: **(el) verbo intransitivo**

A verb which does not require a direct object to complete its meaning.

INTERROGATIVE: **(el) interrogativo**

A form used for asking questions.

INVERSION: **(la) inversión**

Reversal of the normal order of subject and verb.

IRREGULAR VERB: **(el) verbo irregular**

A verb which does not follow one of the regular conjugation patterns.

MOOD: **(el) modo**

The point of view from which an action or statement is seen: factual **(el indicativo)**; subjective, wishful, doubtful, possible, or fearful **(el subjuntivo)**; and commands **(el imperativo)**.

NOUN: **(el) nombre, (el) substantivo**

A word used to name a person, place, quality, or thing.

NUMBER: **(el) número**

Singular or plural.

PAST PARTICIPLE: **(el) participio pasivo**

A form of the verb which indicates time but not the person and is used together with the auxiliary verb **haber** to form all compound tenses. The endings are **-ado** for **-ar** verbs and **-ido** for **-er** and **-ir** verbs.

PLUPERFECT: **(el) pluscuamperfecto**

PREDICATE: **(el) predicado**

The part of a sentence which makes a statement about the subject.

PREPOSITION: **(la) preposición**

A word placed before a noun, pronoun, or verb to show its relationship to some other word in the sentence.

PRESENT PARTICIPLE: (el) gerundio

In Spanish, the present participle may be used only as a verb indicating time but not person, ending in -ando for -ar verbs and -iendo for -er and -ir verbs. The English equivalent ends in -ing.

PRONOUN: (el) pronombre

A word used in place of a noun, an idea, or a group of words.

PUNCTUATION: (la) puntuación

REFLEXIVE VERB: (el) verbo reflexivo

A verb expressing an action in which the subject and the recipient of the action are the same.

RELATIVE PRONOUN: (el) pronombre relativo

A pronoun which joins two clauses. Its antecedent is in the main clause.

SMALL LETTER: (la) minúscula

STEM: (el) radical, (la) raíz

SUBJECT: (el) sujeto

The person or thing that performs an action (active voice) or that receives an action (passive voice).

SUBJUNCTIVE: (el) subjuntivo (See MOOD.)

TENSE: (el) tiempo

The form of a verb which expresses the time of an action.

VERB: (el) verbo

A word which expresses an action or a state of being.

VOICE: (la) voz

active voice:	(la) voz activa	The subject acts.
passive voice:	(la) voz pasiva	The subject is acted upon.

62 Los signos de puntuación

.	**(el) punto**
,	**(la) coma**
;	**(el) punto y coma**
:	**(los) dos puntos**
. . .	**(los) puntos suspensivos**
¿ ?	**(los) signos de interrogación**
¡ !	**(los) signos de admiración**
« »	**(las) comillas**
( )	**(los) paréntesis**
´	**(el) acento escrito**
¨	**(la) diéresis**
~	**(la) tilde**
-	**(el) guión**
—	**(la) raya**

Except for the following differences, Spanish punctuation is much the same as English punctuation.

A. An inverted question mark or exclamation point is placed at the beginning of the interrogative or exclamatory part of the sentence.

> ¿Cómo se llama usted?
> Usted es americano, ¿no es cierto?
> ¡Qué guapa!
> Se salvó la vida, ¡gracias a Dios!

B. To indicate a change of speaker in a dialog, a dash is generally used in Spanish instead of quotation marks.

> —¿Qué le dijiste tú a Juan?
> —Yo no le dije nada.

C.   Arabic numbers are usually punctuated with a period in Spanish. The comma
      is used as a decimal point is in English.

1.000.000	one million
100.000	one hundred thousand
10.000	ten thousand
1.000	one thousand
100	one hundred
1	one
0,1	one tenth
0,01	one hundredth

Index

Numbers in bold-faced type refer to pages. References in parentheses refer to sections.

[233]